D1463032

Of Mother...

Of Mothers and Others

Edited by
JAISHREE MISRA

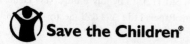

ZUBAAN
an imprint of Kali for Women
128B Shahpur Jat
1st floor
New Delhi 110 049
Email: contact@zubaanbooks.com
www.zubaanbooks.com

First published by Zubaan, 2013
Copyright © this collection, Zubaan and Save the Children, 2013

This publication is supported by Save the Children www.savethechildren.in.

All rights reserved

10 9 8 7 6 5 4 3 2 1

ISBN: 978 93 81017 86 9

Zubaan is an independent feminist publishing house based in New Delhi, India, with a strong academic and general list. It was set up as an imprint of the well known feminist house Kali for Women and carries forward Kali's tradition of publishing world quality books to high editiorial and production standards. 'Zubaan' means tongue, voice, language, speech in Hindustani. Zubaan is a non-profit publisher, working in the areas of the humanities and social sciences, as well as in fiction, general non-fiction, and books for young adults that celebrate difference, diversity and equality, especially for and about the children of India and South Asia under its imprint Young Zubaan.

Typeset in Bembo Std 11.5/15 by Jojy Philip, New Delhi 110 015
Printed at Gopsons Papers Ltd., A-2 & 3, Sector-64, Noida

Contents

Preface

A mother called Birjrunisa in Rajasthan told us how her daughter Tamanna died when she was two-and-a-half because she couldn't take her to the doctor – not just because it was far but also because the family didn't have enough money. Tamanna was suffering from pneumonia and diarrhoea. Her illnesses were treatable – if only Birjrunisa could pay for her treatment.

Her face fell as she recounted the tale of her loss.

Shockingly, this is the prevailing reality of millions in our country. We lose 16.5 lakh children every year – one child every nineteen seconds – in India. In addition, women in India have only a 50/50 chance of anyone skilled to help them give birth and, in most cases, they pay with their lives.

These are not mere statistics but a reflection on how, as a nation and society, we treat our women and children. Poverty is a vicious cycle that pushes people to dire circumstances that we may be oblivious to. Deaths remain uncounted and families learn to cope with loss which becomes an irreversible reality that is beyond their control. The sad truth is that one's chances of survival mostly depend on where one is born and into which strata of society. For the poor, it is the lottery rather that the right to life and survival that determines their future.

Save the Children's campaign against needless child deaths attempts to make this invisible reality visible. We know change is possible. It needs will and a commitment from each one of us to create a nation free of diseases, and a world of equal opportunities for children. Each of us has a role to play.

On behalf of Save the Children, I thank Jaishree Misra who joined us in our efforts to champion this cause. I must also thank Zubaan in taking up this project and getting the book out in time. I thank all the writers whose moving and inspiring pieces form this anthology.

Finally, our hope remains that the efforts will translate into timely political commitments towards mothers and children in our country, and that together we can create a nation where each of them counts. May this project move all its readers, and inspire them to contribute to the positive changes that we seek.

Thomas Chandy
CEO, Save the Children India

Foreword

SHABANA AZMI

India's 'Invisible' Mothers

It is a little known fact that Mumtaz Mahal, Mughul Emperor Shah Jahan's favourite queen died due to complications related to repeated childbirth. For all its beauty, the Taj Mahal is a grim reminder of the fact that, even after 400 years, we seem to have done little to improve the health of the mothers in our country. India continues to hit the headlines because of our shameful record on maternal and child health. UN statistics indicate that in India, a woman dies in childbirth every ten minutes.

On the one hand, India is emerging as a global power and on the other, Save the Children's annual *State of the World's Mothers* table on 'the best place to be a mother' places India 76th out of the 80 middle-income countries listed. In assessing how we look after, educate and offer opportunities to our women and children, we do not come off well. At the same time, India accounts for one fifth of world's burden of child mortality with 1.7 million children dying every year. We lose one child every nineteen seconds: what's worse, most of these deaths can be easily prevented.

The number of women we lose due to pregnancy-related

issues in one week in India is more than in all of Europe in a whole year. In other words, the number of women that we lose in one year in India due to pregnancy-related issues is the same as having 400 plane crashes annually. Can you imagine what would happen if that were the case? Governments would fall. But because in this case it is largely poor rural women who are dying, nobody is paying the slightest attention.

The question arises – are we, as a nation, failing to make women and children count? Or have we simply become numb to large numbers?

I've been campaigning on this issue with Save the Children since 2009. Despite our huge efforts to raise awareness of the daily struggles of families at our very doorstep, there is still a long way to go.

Why are we lagging behind? To be honest, it's hard to know where to fix the blame: we score below average on practically every front. I can't help but notice that our biggest black mark is the fact that women in India have only a 50/50 chance of having anyone skilled to help them during childbirth.

Statistics like this reflect on how, as a nation and a society, how we treat women and girls: how we discriminate against them, disempower them, relegate them to the margins and once they're there, neglect them. We've done this for centuries.

During my visit to a slum in Delhi with Save the Children in 2011, I met women too young to be mothers and health workers who have the tall task of 'changing mindsets' – something that will not happen overnight. One of the crucial areas that Save the Children has been focusing on is the importance of nutrition for both mother and child. Often overlooked, this is in fact the cause of a third of child and a fifth of all maternal deaths. Here again, we are not taking home any prizes. We have the highest rate of child malnutrition of all middle-income countries and the second highest rate in the entire world. A tenth of women in our country are undernourished themselves, and this is being passed on to their newborns from the womb as they start to develop, and on it goes.

The reality is that we are stuck in a vicious cycle. But with political will and increased social awareness, and with the excellent work being done by organsiations such as Save the Children, I believe it is a cycle that can be broken.

Taking care of our women and children builds not just a generation but the nation itself. We neglect mothers at our own peril, at the peril of society. If we are to lead as a nation, we must put our women and children first.

The message needs to reach many more till our society is moved to redress this situation. This anthology is a small step in the right direction.

A little over the year ago, the wheels were set in motion by Jaishree Misra when she pledged her support for Save the Children by undertaking the book that you hold in your hands today. On behalf of Save the Children, I would like to thank Jaishree, the whole team at Zubaan, and everyone who has worked so hard on this project. Thanks to you all, and here's hoping that the book will be a big success.

SHABANA AZMI is an actor and social activist. She is one of the leading ambassadors for Save the Children.

Introduction

JAISHREE MISRA

You would be forgiven for asking: why a book on motherhood? What is there to say on this subject except for the usual platitudes? Becoming a mother is invariably taken as being a joyful experience, longed for and aspired to, especially in India, where childlessness carries a stigma worse perhaps than widowhood.

It started with an event organised by Save the Children where I found myself promising to edit a book that would highlight the problems some women face in caring for their children. Rash, yes, but I had been staggered to find that, in India, we lose a child every nineteen seconds to easily preventable diseases and it seemed worth trying to help the organisation employ more health workers to assist struggling families. In such instances, books are my preferred currency because they are more likely to change perceptions than all the money in the world.

Typically, on reflection, I found myself in a state of panic. Publishers have good reason to shy away from 'worthy' books, which are usually considered unsaleable. However, there are fortunately still a small handful of publishers around, like Zubaan, who, despite the many difficulties, find ingenious ways to continue producing material that pushes boldly at all such boundaries. Zubaan came up with an enthusiastic offer of publication which was accompanied – almost like a good portent – by an excellent ready-made piece on the relationship between food and mothering by editor, Anita Roy. As we excitedly pooled names of writer friends at that first meeting, I could start to see an anthology that would overturn all those glib presumptions about motherhood that are churned out by commerce and advertising. Yes, of course, the subject would be celebratory for those whose experience of this gift has been positive. But – if I were to stay true to my original promise – this would also be a book that would startle people out of their complacency, even if only to have them accept that motherhood isn't always the comforting, 'cuddly' experience we like to think it is. Not that I enjoy upsetting cherished notions but this is one way to help readers glance, for a moment, into the abyss that some women stare at every day.

Our guideline to contributors was this: '*Anything* that examines the subject of motherhood is welcome: an essay or short story or poem. First, second, third person, comic, tragic, soft, savage… pick your style and be as bold as you like because it is exactly this variation in experience that we need to convey.'

In the hands of talented writers, this was sure to open all sorts of windows. And, to our delight, the response was overwhelming. Almost everyone immediately had an opinion, an idea, a story; some wanted to waive even the token payments that were on offer, given Zubaan's excellent credentials and because this was an awareness and fundraising initiative. What astonished me further, as articles and stories started to gather in my mail-box, was the honesty with which everyone seemed willing to tackle such a personal subject. I hope readers are as comforted by some of the pieces as I was, my own feelings about motherhood being mixed at the best of times. I should explain.

Motherhood came early in my own life, following an arranged marriage while I was still in my teens. I was too young and too confused to cope at all well with cloth diapers and colic and swiftly turned into one of those anxious young mums my heart now goes out to. I'd had my child at the wrong time and for all the wrong reasons and when, a few months later, it also emerged that she was mentally challenged, I thought, aged twenty-three, that life had ended. But I grew to love my daughter with fierce protectiveness and, as the years passed, it was the prejudices she faced that catalysed me to take on and change many things that a more 'normal' kind of motherhood might have shackled me to. Essentially, she freed me from society's expectations – a test which I had apparently failed anyway by having her at all – and so I got a divorce, rediscovered my first love, moved to England, became both a working woman and a novelist, and embraced life in all its fullness. Paradoxically, it would seem, motherhood became the driving force in my liberation as a woman.

Then, just as I finally started to enjoy my daughter, came a series of miscarriages. Four incomplete babies followed each other, all in the space of five years. It looked like motherhood wasn't meant for me without all sorts of attendant heartache. These were the years when I was in England and much help was at hand in the form of solicitous nurses, self-help groups, a sweet-faced social worker who talked to us in a beguiling voice about the possibility of adoption. My husband and I were open to the idea, but were sure we only wanted a baby from India, partly because children of Asian origin hardly ever come up on the Adoption Register in Britain and we could have languished forever on a waiting list, no doubt growing increasingly desperate. This was when we found that British Home Office rules at the time carried a price tag of six-thousand pounds for overseas adoptions. It wasn't parting with the money that worried us but, having spent most of our lives in India, we both knew of the circumstances under which most children end up in orphanages and six-thousand pounds was certainly a sum large enough to keep such a child in her own natural home for some considerable time. I wasn't sure I could comfortably become mother to a child by the mere good fortune of having more money than her biological mother did and so, rightly or wrongly, that door was closed without further consideration. Doubts about whether we had made the right decision stayed with me for a long time and I have to say that the pieces on adoption in this book made me re-focus my thoughts to a great degree.

Nevertheless, I learnt along the way to deal positively with this set-back. I stopped counting in my head the ages my miscarried brood would have been: the youngest, fifteen this year and, my goodness, the oldest would have been twenty! Quite probably a college student, bringing home dirty laundry, slouching on the sofa, mumbling a lot and finding fault with his father all the time. If it did come up in our conversation, my husband and I would laugh wryly and – mostly – we genuinely stopped minding. I learnt to derive joy rather than envy from the successes of friends' children and the more generous of them freely gave me access to their rites of passage. Vicariously, thus, I too heard the gushings of puppy love, tasted the charred results of cooking experiments, lived through the stress of board exams and college admissions, and experienced that motherly heart-in-mouth moment at first mention of back-packing adventures in places I hadn't even heard of.

I also found various imaginative ways to continue ducking my army of fond aunts who gamely carried on, well into my middle-age, pressing details of this gynaecologist or that swami on me, insisting that my marriage was incomplete and shaky without the glue of children.

That I found was simply not true. Being an observer, I'd already noted how much easier it was for couples who did not have offspring to enjoy each other and life's rich offerings; there's one couple in particular I can think of who would need a pick-axe to prise them apart. And it isn't merely relationships but many other things that can be enhanced by childlessness too: creativity, for one, and a social consciousness that's so much harder when one's own must naturally take precedence over anyone else. I don't often state this openly because, in India, such protestations from women who are not conventional mothers are either scoffed at or seen as disingenuous and trying too hard. Hence my delight when Urvashi Butalia, my editorial colleague on this book and a woman who enjoys an extraordinarily rich and varied life herself, offered to write a piece about her decision to remain childless. In mirroring what that has meant to her with the maternal yearnings and disappointments of a variety of friends, Urvashi gave me a thoughtful and candid essay that explores childlessness in both its heartbreaking and potentially fulfilling aspects.

However (and I quote Jane Austen here, who was also too intelligent to be enamoured by the complexities of motherhood), 'despite all my resolutions on the side of self-government, I found myself unable, with an inability almost physical,' to stay away from motherhood when it came to my writing. My novels have dealt with several aspects of this huge subject: maternal loss, maternal love, bereavement, adoption, rejection... I wondered if this was peculiar to me, the convolutions of my mothering life being the cause. So what sweet relief when writer after writer I worked with on this book said almost exactly the same thing: that, for them, motherhood had always either been a relentless force in their own writing or a recurring theme. Surprisingly, other descriptions emerged too, within the safety of emails: motherhood was a 'surprisingly dark obsession', one that had 'weighed down' the writing or 'underpinned the sub-conscious'... One writer told me about the difficult relationship she had had with her own mother. Mere days after sending out my initial exploratory email, I knew I had the makings of a layered and thought-provoking book.

Of course, the Zubaan team and I were very sure that we did not want to lose sight of the most joyous aspects of motherhood – and Jahnavi Barua's tenderly evocative essay on being a doctor and marveling at the changes in her physical body while expecting her first child is testament to that. But it remained an important objective to reveal as many different facets of this fascinating subject without slipping into conceits and contrivances.

Shashi Deshpande's reflective study of motherhood using literature, mythology and her own experiences was one of the first pieces I received, setting a bench-mark of quality that the rest of the anthology was going to have to live up to. Like unexpected gifts, however, they kept coming.

The first piece of fiction was Shinie Anthony's story about a woman despairing over never being able to have children, an experience many readers will identify with, here undercut with unexpected humour and a life-affirming ending.

There were further dollops of fun, for anyone who has parented knows that it's impossible to do this without being able to laugh. I cannot offer a better vehicle to enjoy a roller-coaster ride past some depictions of motherhood than Jai Arjun Singh's masterful essay on Hindi cinema's mothers through the ages. Bulbul Sharma's plea on behalf of modern-day globe-trotting grandmas and Smriti Lamech's inversion of that familiar Indian longing for a male child with her personal desire to have a girl also prodded me into thinking of this subject laterally rather than literally.

Yet, revealing just how searing some experiences of motherhood can be, I read about the lingering anguish of mothers of 'disappeared' boys in Kashmir whom Humra Quraishi met in her years of journalistic writings on the Valley. And went on to feel the pain of surrogate mothers whose wombs are hired out to wealthy childless couples, one of whose stories is starkly unveiled in N. B. Sarojini and Vrina Marwah's scholarly article on the work they do with SAMA.

We also contacted a journalist I knew to be fearless and principled whose writings on the painful issue of abusive mothers I had read and admired in the past. Under the nom de plume of Prabha Walker, she sent in a piece that examines this difficult and rarely-discussed subject with unusual compassion and empathy.

Fellow fiction writers, Kishwar Desai, Sarita Mandanna and Nisha Susan, also got straight to the nub of the particular requirement of this collection, producing a brilliant trio of stories that resonated excitingly with each other. Perhaps it is fiction that is best placed among all the arts to make possible the seemingly impossible. But here, three times over, the reader will get caught up in some of the darkest deeds mothers are capable of and I would ask only for you to imagine (as, indeed as one of the stories asks), what you would do cast in the same position as these luckless women.

Two vibrant and talented poets — Meena Alexander and Tishani Doshi — also sent in contributions traversing subjects as tragic as foeticide and abandonment. Always a little envious of the craft of poetry, I could only marvel at how mere words, when strung together with such skill, transcended the normal language of heartbreak.

Adoption was a necessary part of such a varied exploration. Mridula Koshy's short story takes a bold and unusually ambivalent view of the adoption of a baby, pointing at some of the lows, while a true-life first person account came in from someone (given the pseudonym here of Andromeda Nebula) who, in adopting a sibling pair of older children, reveals the patience and hard work that goes into earning this sometimes difficult love. And what can one say on that most poignant subject of loss? What happens to parents when their children die; how do they ever pull themselves up from such a devastating body-blow to face the curiosity of the world again? I will forever be overcome by admiration for Manju Kapur who, having lost a beautiful and beloved twenty-one-year-old daughter, and held a dignified silence on the subject all these years, bravely agreed to write for the first time about this experience in the hope of offering comfort to other mothers in similar situations.

Which led me to consider the loss of our own mothers to death or dementia... that inevitable and saddening prospect to those of us who have been blessed with maternal love. Shalini Sinha, who was contributing a piece on bringing up her intellectually challenged son, lost her own mother (and son's primary carer) just as she started writing her piece. But dogged persistence in the face of grief is a characteristic I'm familiar with in my many years of observing special needs parents. Shalini submitted her piece on time, a heartfelt and ruminative essay on bereavement and grief and ultimate acceptance.

It seemed fitting to end such a courageous collection with Namita Gokhale's wistful and poetic piece on Kunti, the most complex mother figure the great epics have given us, who – despite giving birth to heroes and warriors begotten by gods – was forever tortured by the memory of the baby she gave away. It is in that ancient story most of all that we may ultimately understand those women whom Save the Children – and this book – are seeking to help.

I thank you for your support in buying this anthology and hope you benefit from reading it as much as I did bringing it to you.

September 2012
New Delhi

Determination

Smriti Lamech

'A son is a son till he gets him a wife, a daughter's a daughter, all her life.' Brought up by a fiercely feminist grandmother, I could say that line in my sleep by the time I was two. Despite coming from a conservative little town in Uttar Pradesh, I was moulded to believe that all civilisation began and ended with women, brainwashed in a way that would do jihadis proud. My grandmother didn't know she was feminist, of course, and would turn in her grave if she were to hear me describe her so. Delicate, petite, fine-featured and almost bashful at first sight, my grandmother was the epitome of steel claws sheathed in velvet paws. Hers was a rather matriachal family, and like most Bengali women, she believed firmly that a home, and the world in general, were better off run by the fairer sex. Men would do better to just leave it all in the capable hands of their women and simply follow orders – just as the Good Lord intended. The Good Lord, of course, was a He and years after she passed away I wondered how a male Almighty fitted into her worldview. But I digress.

I played Estella to her Miss Havisham and, while I wonder if it was conscious on her part, I was soon quite convinced that men were irrelevant, dispensable, incidental. It was not a bitter indoctrination by any means. Simply, her deep and unshakeable conviction that she passed on to me, almost like a legacy, along with the family china and her diamond and ruby set hoops. Women nurtured life within them, they were compassionate, they were wise, they were capable of deep feelings while men had the emotional depth of a demitasse spoon. In fact, she'd hint delicately, trying to gloss over the birds and bees chapter of my education, that men were only good for one thing. And once you were done with that, it was best to leave them watching football while you got on with the business of raising your daughter. Naturally, we'd give birth to daughters. Strong women in our own image. Women who would rule the world. It was important to create independent, free women in a country like ours. We didn't need boys. We could get enough of those when we needed them and then ignore them.

It wasn't just what she said: it was the way she led by example. A double MA, she went on to appear for the civil service exams, this just after Independence when her contemporaries were mostly Britishers. She founded two schools and was an artist and writer. One of the few women of her time who got married at the late age of twenty-five when most of her friends were wedded and bedded by sixteen. It wasn't for lack of admirers though. It was because she decided to look after her ageing parents, her one condition during courtship being that my grandfather agree to move into her ancestral home instead of the other way around. Her sisters were equally fiery, intelligent and independent, one the principal of a college, another the

Inspectoress of Education (a term long-since forgotten) and yet another, trained with Elizabeth Arden, going on to become a beauty consultant for airlines. All of them equally determined career women, fiery, despite their crisp cottons and chiffon sarees, faces sans make-up and wearing a single strand of pearls. Years later when my mother began to set up one successful business after the other, selling them off when bored to pick up something absolutely new, my husband jokingly coined a term for her: serial entrepreneur. Yes, the women in my family were strong role models and, even if I didn't particularly live up to their stellar examples, I knew that one day, I wanted to contribute to this long line of illustrious women with my own little firebrand.

Years later as I stood there holding the home test in my hands and the two confirmatory lines slowly appeared, I felt a surge of adrenaline run through my system. In a few months time I'd be holding my baby girl! If it weren't for the fact that I'd just peed on it, I might have kissed the little plastic chip.

But before I'd even had my first check-up, the litany started: 'We'd like a grandson,' said my father-in-law. Umm, yes, of course, I said, feeling like a waitress missing her notepad while taking down an order. Almost everyone we met assumed we'd want a boy. 'Because he's your first child,' 'You need an heir for the family name,' 'He'll be the elder son of the elder son', 'A boy is one's security for old age'. The more they said it, the more I mentally dug in my heels: it was a girl. She just *had* to be.

I lay at the ultrasound centre with my shirt pulled up under my breasts, my still flat belly covered in goosebumps as they spread the cold jelly on it. The doctor placed the transducer on my stomach and I held my breath. This was it! *This* was it? A dot? Maybe it wasn't a baby at all, maybe that was just a speck of dust on the screen. I screwed up my eyes and watched as the doctor peered and blinked at the screen for what seemed like an age. Carpe diem, I thought and grabbing my courage with both hands, I said, 'Can you tell if it's a girl yet? He turned around and said a little too sharply, 'Well, right now we can't even be sure if it's a baby; it could be just a cyst. You've come too early. And you do know that it's illegal to disclose the gender, don't you?'

I collected my clothes and dignity and left. Did I look like the sort of person who'd harm my child, I grumbled all the way back, while my husband did his best to soothe me and tell me that it wasn't personal, they were just doing their job.

A few days later, a second scan confirmed that the dot was, indeed, a baby. I tried my luck again, asking the nurse who wiped the gel off my belly, 'Is it a girl?' She pretended she'd got something in her eye and then became totally absorbed in getting the gel out of my navel. I was getting no answers here.

My baby bump refused to grow into a real bump and that should have been a cause for concern, but it wasn't. I was puking my guts out before and after every meal, but I couldn't care less. All I wanted was a confirmation that the cause was indeed a female one. It would all be worth it, just to hold my baby girl in my arms. She'd be everything I wanted to be but had never really managed to be: brave, strong, intelligent, feisty, fearless, funny, fabulous, a paragon of virtue really, without being particularly virtuous.

Around my sixth month, my husband had to travel abroad for two months. By this time my gynaecologist had confirmed that I was terribly underweight and needed better care. So it was decided that I would be deposited with my parents while my husband was away, a ewe being fattened up to deliver a lamb, as it were.

A new city, a new gynae, a new opportunity to pump the technician for info. Surely this was a sign! God wanted to give me the opportunity to get the nurse to confirm what I already *knew*: that my baby was a girl.

And not a moment did I waste. The moment the doctor finished and walked out, leaving the nurse to clean me up, I turned to her, the world in my eyes, begging, pleading – Is it a girl? She looked around worriedly. She could lose her job over this. Then she bent down and whispered, as though she was letting me into the secret of eternal youth, '*Bachcha hai.*' I looked at her in bewilderment. Of course it was a baby. But was it a girl or a boy? Looking at the confusion writ large on my face she tried again, '*Bachcha hai… bachcha*'. I smiled weakly, thanked her for informing me that the thing in my belly was in fact a baby and and not a pot of yoghurt, straightened my clothes and left.

Running out of time and options, I tried the good old Chinese calendar. It predicted a male child. Shutting the website in frustration, I hunted down our old family retainer. She was known for her ability to predict a baby's gender and for all the years I had doubted that ability, I was ready to eat humble pie. She looked at my face, examined the huge bump I was lugging around, asked me what I felt like eating and after some thought, delivered her verdict: a boy. My heart sank. I was now scraping the bottom of the barrel when I got an aunt to do the old wedding-ring–on-a-gold-chain trick. The answer stayed the same: boy.

My family couldn't fathom why I was not content to wait, why the mystery was eating away at me. 'I just want to know so that I can shop for baby clothes,' I said, lamely. 'Why can't you just wait to find out the way we all did?' said my mother, ever practical and brusque. '*Because*' was my rather mature response as I waddled out with as much dignity as my considerable bulk allowed.

At some level I was well aware of how unreasonable it was to yearn so much for a girl. What good reason can there ever be to specifically want a child of either gender? But then as humans, our evolutionary fitness is measured by the children we leave behind and the desire to leave something behind in your own image is natural, if slightly egotistical. And I wanted a daughter 'in my own image,' I suppose. Besides, I wouldn't know what to do with a creature that came with external plumbing, I told myself, and surely nature wouldn't give a mother something she wasn't equipped to handle. Fraternising with the oppressors was bad enough, giving birth to one was unthinkable. I wanted a girl, needed a girl, deserved a girl, and would accept nothing less than a girl. Biology be damned – the baby would be what I willed it to be.

And then suddenly, before I knew it, time was up. The baby wasn't faring too well and I needed a caesarean the next day. It wasn't the impending open surgery that kept me up all night. It was the realisation that this was the end of hope. It would be what it would be, and there was absolutely nothing I could do about it.

As I lay on the operating table, I let my mind wander. It helped distract me from the humiliation of being treated like a block of wood. They'd left me naked under a harsh light and I figured the air-conditioning would kill me before the embarrassment did. Either way, it would also soon be over, and I'd have my prize, my daughter. The anaesthetic wouldn't set in and even as they began to slice me open I wriggled my toes and writhed in terror. But I was okay, this was all going to be okay, because (say it with me) I'd get my little baby girl at the end of it all. Rough hands pressed chloroform on a rag down over my face and I clutched at consciousness as it slipped away. The incision was made and the baby couldn't be prised out because the head was too big, I heard them say. A hundred hands were on me, some pressing down on my chest, some holding down my flailing arms, others moving within my body, pulling, pulling. Pulling my unwilling baby out of my body.

Later on, I'd look back and wonder if my little baby boy felt hurt and rejection. Did he know how badly I wanted a girl? Then I'd laugh at my foolish notions. But right then, my baby refused to give up the safety of the womb. I stopped counting and took deep breaths to calm myself, even as the hands invaded me. I'd never felt so violated, so eviscerated. Then I heard the baby wail. I was too tired to talk and too scared to ask. The exhaustion of the last few hours got to me and I passed out, not knowing even then, what it was.

I woke up after what felt like hours but was all of ten minutes. 'Is it a girl?' I asked, my feeble voice unrecognisable even to myself. Hands busily worked at my stomach, piecing me back together, sewing up the womb they'd ripped my baby out of. No one bothered to answer. I was merely the woman who had given birth. I didn't warrant a response.

I asked again.

'You can relax, it's a boy,' said one of them gruffly. They'd blindfolded me when I came in for the surgery (so that I couldn't watch the surgery and writhe in fear) and I felt the tears run down my cheeks before I realised I was crying. My wrists were tied to a board slipped under my shoulders and I couldn't wipe my eyes. I'm not sure how much time passed before I ventured (and I plead extreme terror, exhaustion, youth and anaesthesia, here), 'Can't you exchange him for a baby girl?'

There was a minute of shocked, deafening silence, and then the room exploded in a cacophony of angry voices. 'This is not that sort of hospital!', 'Are you insane?', 'What an ungrateful woman', 'And such a fair baby boy too', 'Such women don't deserve boys', 'Why does God bless women like her with sons?' This is a small town in Uttar Pradesh. In this dusty little place where wanting a daughter is unheard of, rejecting a son is sacrilege. Babies are exchanged at birth, female foetuses are aborted, infant girls are found tied up in plastic bags at the garbage dumps, pigs rooting around them. I had just committed the worst sort of sin by not appreciating my good fortune in having a male child.

Through a fog of anaesthesia, the harsh voices washed over me. I lay there, detached, blind, tired. It was over. A lifetime of wanting a baby, nine months of carrying one, wishing and hoping it was a girl. And now, it was over. I had a son.

In snatches I recalled the nurse who had whispered to me '*Bachcha hai*'. Belatedly, I realised she meant it was a male child. I wished I'd understood and begun to make my peace with the fact, then.

I felt a hospital gown being pulled over my body. The air-conditioning had long ceased to bother me and I was numb for so many reasons, in so many ways. I felt myself being lifted on to a wheeled stretcher and trundling down a corridor, voices echoing around me. I was still blindfolded. After a while there was stillness, silence and a much desired peace. I lay there and waited, drifting in and out of consciousness. Time flowed gently over me and I could have been lying there for minutes, hours or days.

A familiar voice said my name. It was my guardian angel in the guise of a friend who knew her way around doctors and hospitals and procedures. The baby had been taken to the private room where my family was waiting over an hour ago. And I'd been rolled into a deserted corridor and abandoned, for daring to voice such heresy. Punished for my blasphemy.

She took off my blindfold, clucked over the marks it had left on my face and wheeled me back to the ward, cursing the nursing staff all the way. Thunderous applause and cheers greeted me as I was rolled into the room. Friends and family had gathered to welcome my son into this world. I lay there, feeling no joy, no elation, just exhaustion. And then I exhaled.

They held him up to me, swaddled in a little printed sheet. His beady eyes appraised me, met mine unblinkingly. I stared at him and told myself this was the moment I was supposed to fall in love with my baby. But I couldn't. A couple of hours passed in slow motion. People laughing, grandparents crying tears of joy, the bundle being passed from lap to lap.

Finally he was handed to me to nurse. I looked at him dispassionately. I was tired, disappointed, resentful and clueless about nursing. I'd just got my body back and it was already time to share it with this… this boy child. I wish I could say I put him to my breast and fell in love. But I didn't. I wish I could say I fell in love with his long eyelashes as he fell asleep in the crook of my arm. But I didn't. I wish I could say the curve of his nose, so identical to mine, made me feel a surge of love. But it didn't. This child had arrived, and with his arrival, dashed my hopes of a daughter. I wasn't feeling particularly charitable towards him, but I'd do my duty nonetheless, I promised myself.

And then one morning, many days later, I woke up and, through the mists of sleep, I reached out for him instinctively. I held him with the early rays of the sun streaming in and the emotion hit me with the force of a ten-tonne truck. My son. My precious, precious baby.

SMRITI LAMECH went on to be a more accepting mother than her piece suggests, to the point of quitting full-time work and freelancing because she couldn't bear to let her son and then her daughter (yes, she had one, after him!) out of her sight. She loves her garden, her fridge full of chocolate, her teetering stacks of books and her lily pond, all of which she appreciates thoroughly when she is not busy fighting deadlines. A prolific blogger, she has strong opinions and likes to wear her feminist badge on her sleeve.

On the Other Side

JAHNAVI BARUA

I thought I could not be better prepared for pregnancy and childbirth and all that lay on the other side. After all, I was a doctor and had been studying the mysteries of the human body for years now; none of its inner workings was mysterious to me. From the moment I woke up until the hour I went to sleep, I was aware of what my body was up to, in a manner a lay person could not comprehend. I knew well that sophisticated, complex system – the endocrine system – that controlled the ticking of the body as skilfully and elegantly as the conductor of an orchestra: it silently released the chemicals known as hormones, on time and in the exact quantities needed to initiate cascading actions that ensured my body worked as efficiently as it was meant to. If I felt more tired than usual, I would pause – only for a fleeting moment – to consider if my thyroid gland was functioning under par; if I experienced difficulty falling asleep, I would wonder if my pineal gland was giving trouble. The heart, the lungs, the kidneys, I understood intimately what they were doing as they went about their daily business.

This is not to say I dwelt inordinately on these things – I certainly was not a hypochondriac: rather, I was careless, cavalier even, as far my health was concerned – but I had a knowledge of the human body that I enjoyed, was in awe of and relished. The central nervous system especially – the brain, the spinal cord – enthralled me. Here was an organ where biology worked together with physics and chemistry to create a structure more sophisticated than can be imagined. Consider, for instance, the small fact of how chewing slowly affected the satiety centre in the ventromedial nucleus of the hypothalamus: if one chewed slowly taking longer over a morsel of food a larger number of nervous impulses arrived at the centre than if one ate rapidly, thus lulling the centre into believing one was full. An effortlessly simple way to lose a little bit of extra weight. This was the kind of minutiae about the human body that I relished.

When the pregnancy test showed up positive, ten days after a missing period, I thought, with awe, of how the embryo had already been through so much frenetic activity without my knowledge. Silently, secretly, the fertilised egg had divided, first into two and then exponentially, forming a solid ball of cells called the morula, a structure reminiscent of the fruit of the mulberry. After three days in the uterine tube, it had made its way into the uterine cavity. The embryo – it would be called an embryo for another four weeks when it officially became a foetus – had implanted itself into the uterine wall, digging roots deep into its newly lush soil. This tiny creature, smaller than a sesame seed, had already embarked on its epic journey helped along by my subversive body and I hadn't even known. Somehow, I had believed, with my superior knowledge I would know when my womb transformed itself into a nest for a young one. The thought that I had been completely peripheral to this cataclysmic event in my life was a sobering one. In the days to come, nature persisted in telling me how redundant I was.

As I went about my normal life, the embryo took charge of its own fortunes: with little help from me, it commenced organogenesis, the act of forming specialised organs from its cells. The brain, spinal cord, the heart and the gastrointestinal tract were now being built. And to humiliate me further, to emphasise that book learning or even patient care could never be a substitute for the real thing, it struck me down with morning sickness. As I retched in response to all kinds of smells and tastes – daal boiling in the pressure cooker being one of the main culprits – I swore never again to take lightly the complaints of pregnant women. Where I had dismissed their querulous protestations earlier, I now fell into deep sympathy with their lot.

By the time, the storm of morning sickness had quietened three months had passed. More in control of my body – or so, I thought – I took stock of the situation. The foetus, now about three inches long, would have begun producing bile in its miniature liver; the circulatory system would be taking shape and so would the urinary. While the foetus had grown so had I, assuming a round plumpness that perplexed me every time I looked in the mirror. The sterile facts of weight gain per month as laid out in textbooks and as evinced by pregnant women in hospital was made real as clothes stopped fitting and new curves established themselves. This new adventure was turning into something tangible after all.

As I shuffled across from the first trimester into the second, an event occurred that finally threw all that I had read and studied and practised out of the window. Close to the end of the sixteenth week, I felt a flutter in my abdomen; a very gentle movement as if someone or something was moving softly, reaching out for someone. Many times, we had read in our textbooks, assigning the fact to memory in case questioned in an oral examination, that the first foetal movement could be discerned in the sixteenth to twentieth weeks, an event known as quickening. This precious moment is often missed as women attribute it to gas or a normal intestinal movement, but I was fortunate; I understood it for what it was. When I felt that first tentative movement, I experienced an immediate reflexive transformation of my own: no longer did I think in terms of embryos and foetuses; all I could think of now was the baby. My baby. I had crossed over to the other side. Willingly, eagerly, I relinquished my rank in the medical fraternity and joined the countless mothers that had gone before me and the ones that would follow.

At the ultrasound examination, when I saw my child's foot for the first time – it was a big one and my son still has big feet – I was dumbstruck. The sight of his little spine furled up like a fiddle-head fern, something I had seen many times before in other ultrasounds, overwhelmed me. A baby was a miracle. I had heard this many times before – all of us have – but just how profound a miracle, how immense, sunk in now. For the journey a baby embarks upon is a remarkably perilous one. From the moment the zygote – the fertilised cell – is formed it begins its fight for survival. There are so many things that can go wrong and do go wrong. To begin with, the nest – the uterine lining and wall – have to cooperate; under the influence of hormones thrown out furiously by something called the Corpus Luteum and subsequently, the placenta, its lining grows thicker and more vascular than before; the muscular walls hypertrophy in preparation for the mammoth task of delivering the child into the outside world. At the same time, other hormones work to ensure they do not contract before they have to; if they did, the baby would be lost. Having settled firmly into the uterus, the growing foetus has to ensure all its organs, all its tissues, limbs have to develop perfectly. A precarious situation when something as minute as low folic acid – a vitamin – in the mother's blood could result in developmental malformation of the baby's brain. Inch by inch, the baby grows and matures and in the end, has to negotiate a hazardous journey out of the womb into the outside world. Yet, for thousands of years this has been the most natural of processes in nature and this cycle of reproduction has ensured that the human race has travelled so far.

A strange peace engulfed me as I watched, on the screen, my son lying curled up, his oversized foot stuck out as if in greeting. From that day on, I surrendered all my fear, my apprehensions and took fiercely to a blind motherhood instead. On humid still summer afternoons, I lay on my back, waiting for that kick that signalled my child greeting me, I did not bother to count the kicks as I earlier would have; I tucked into tangy mango pickles throwing to the wind all thoughts of gastritis or reflux oesophagitis the spicy pickle would induce later. Chatting to the baby all the time, I put together his layette: the little vests with ties and not buttons, for buttons would hurt the delicate skin; sleepsuits with giraffes and lions gambolling all over them; a mobile that turned slowly to the tune of 'Twinkle, Twinkle Little Star'. I have never felt more hopeful and joyous than in those slow days as I waited for my child to arrive. There is a strange comfort in surrendering to nature, I discovered in those sweet days, a comfort more powerful than all the scientific knowledge in the world.

In the final hours, wracked by pain, held tight in the terrible vice of uterine contractions, I did not fight the assault. Letting go of all fear, of all that I had studied about the three stages of labour and all the perils along the stages, I submitted to the natural energy that had carried women through this ordeal; it was a long night, there were moments of despair, moments of absolute wonder but surmounting all that was a breathless anticipation, a hunger that was sated only when I held my son in my arms, in the pale light of dawn. As the sun rose on a new day, I held the precious bundle in my arms. He was as heavy as the universe yet as light as the tears on my cheeks. A precious thing indeed, a child was; I found out that night just how precious. Along with that revelation, I also discovered how science, having given us so much, still could not prepare us, sometimes, for real life. On the other side of the fence was a mysterious world where much remained to be explained.

Motherhood changes all of us. Overnight, it makes women out of girls, a new maturity arriving unannounced at their doorsteps. Timid, tentative girls are transformed into assertive, fierce women when they assume this new role. For me, the change was in another direction altogether. From relying steadfastly on science, on the workings of the human body as I had been taught it, I had relaxed into someone who did not always stop to examine and analyze, but paused to savour those priceless moments: the first step the child took, the thousand-watt smile that lit up the room and my life; the first garbled word the child spoke one rainy morning. I had been allowed the privilege of stepping into another world altogether and I have held on firmly to that, ever since.

JAHNAVI BARUA is a writer based in Bangalore. Her first book, a collection of short fiction, *Next Door*, was published by Penguin in December 2008 to wide critical acclaim. Her second book, a novel, *Rebirth*, was shortlisted for the Man Asian Literary Prize 2011 and for the Commonwealth Book Prize 2012. In her fiction, Jahnavi explores the complex world of human relationships; she is fascinated by what flows beneath the surface of human interaction. Another aspect she examines in her work is the concept of the outsider, literally and otherwise. A strong sense of place marks Jahnavi's fiction; her native Assam and Bangalore find their way often into her fiction. Jahnavi has an eleven-year-old son.

Eating Baby

Anita Roy

'[The fetus] is composed of five elements; he has
everything he needs. His *buddhi* (consciousness) is
fivefold and because he is conscious, he has knowledge
of perfumes and flavors... Then, due to what he has
become, because of what he has eaten and drunk, fed
by his mother through the body's canals and [umbilical]
cord, his breath takes on vigor.'

Garbha-Upanisad (Upanisad of the Embryo),
transl. Lakshmi Kapani

Five minutes after my baby was born, he was nestled
against my breast, suckling. It seemed the least I could
do to help ease the traumatic passage from inner to outer
world. It was a way of saying: 'Don't worry. We may be
separated, but you're not alone.' This, before the milk even
starts to kick in, must be the first ever instance of 'comfort
food'. I immediately empathised with him: 'The world may
be big and weird and loud, but at least there are Mars bars.'
(Or, in his case, ma's bras).

Later, as I watched the grey dawn slowly lighten the
clean square of the hospital window, it occurred to me that
the only people who need 'nursing' when they're not ill,

are babies. It's a word that encompasses care and food, as though gestation is a period of illness that they need help to get over, that their early days and months of life are spent recuperating. The faint whiff of hospital beds, linoleum floors, and disinfectant clings to even the healthiest baby. I watched a new mother in the bed across the corridor pick up her tiny baby from her clear plastic tub, holding her as gingerly as an unexploded grenade. Extreme youth and extreme age are potent reminders of the closeness of death; the wall between life and its opposite is so permeable – as thin as a membrane, as quiet as a heartbeat. Babies, like the very sick, or the very old, precipitate a protective terror in their carers – a kind of constant vigilance to ward off the spectre of unbeing. And our chief weapon in that war (us mothers, that is) is food.

It's no coincidence that the root of the word 'nurse' is the Latin *nutrire*, to nourish – the same as that for 'nurture'. After all, 'Cake', as a friend once announced to me, shoving some my way, 'equals love'. And is there any more basic expression of love than the desire to nourish someone – either physically, by piling another helping onto their plate, or emotionally or spiritually, tending them so that they may flourish?

Nursing the baby, it was impossible not to somehow enact or embody an idea. A mother feeding a baby *means* love. The image is one of the principal icons of the Christian faith. The 'milk of human kindness' is the kind that I was producing, not what's left on your doorstep every morning. Apart from all the metaphorical resonances, it was a brilliant system: no sterilising, no cups and spoons and spillage, no mess, no equipment, no heating up, no cooling down – and just the right amount every time. It seemed as though God were trying to make up for the serious design flaws in the earlier 'giving birth' part of the process (didn't anyone tell him to make this thing *wider*?).

The digestive system of a newborn baby is very much a work in progress. Able to cope only with breastmilk – or its man-made equivalent – at first, the baby's stomach and intestines slowly develop the capacity to process more complex foods. This sounds like a smooth and untroubled process, but anyone who has heard the screaming agony of a baby with colic knows it isn't so. At this stage in life, the workings of the digestive system are epic and all-consuming: there is no greater trial than getting a reluctant baby to suckle, no greater triumph than the production of a burp.

Over the months, the baby and I settled into the cosy yin-yang of breastfeeding. Rooted to the spot, cradling his head, stranded on the island of Mamababy, self-sufficient yet utterly dependent, I tried my best to avoid thinking about weaning. I've never been much of a cook, and the idea that I would have to prepare and feed this child for days and weeks and years to come filled me with alarm. Maybe, I thought to myself, I can go on breastfeeding him until he's ready to go to restaurants and order for himself.

I put off the fateful day, taking grim comfort in babycare guru Gina Ford's warnings that introducing solids too early can not only 'put pressure on [the baby's] liver and kidneys and impair his digestive system,' but may also increase the risk of asthma, eczema and hay fever. Persistent coughing is more common in babies who have been given solids early, and if that wasn't enough to put the fear of god into you, she concludes with the cheery thought that 'early weaning can lead to overfeeding, making the baby too fat, which… can lead to obesity in later life and increase the risk of cancer, diabetes, heart disease, etc.'

I had initially decided that we'd start him on solids after exactly four months. But was that too soon? By being too hasty, would I condemn my precious bundle to a tragic early death after a short life spent scratching, sneezing and wheezing? There again, if I left it too late, then he might not get the vital nutrients he needs at this stage. He might – god forbid! – get *hungry*. In motherhood, as in comedy, timing is everything.

And what about hygiene? Would his first lovin' spoonful be an introduction to the wonderful world of food or a dreadful bout of botulism? Into our Garden of Eden, a snake was about to enter – and the forbidden fruit, in this case, would have to be boiled and mashed.

###

Finally, I could put it off no longer. If this were a film, this is where the screen would fill with pages of a calendar being ripped off by a rushing wind, slowing to a halt around early November, and dissolving to a shot of a hazy Delhi dawn.

As I keeled onto my side towards the baby, I realised how it was these pauses in the days' hectic rush, lying down as he suckled, that had given a structure to our time, had given my days a grammar and shape; my bracket curved around his apostrophe. Although I was determined to keep on breastfeeding him for a while at least, that particular morning felt valedictory. When I was pregnant, he was what I ate; until today, I was what he ate. From now on, he would slowly be made up of something else...

I cannot remember why I decided on cauliflower as his first ever taste sensation, but cauliflower it was: a perfect white floret, a cumulus nimbus of nutrients just waiting to be ingested. But before it could be boiled, the saucepan needed to be thoroughly scrubbed. But before it could be scrubbed, the scrubber had to be boiled. Which, of course, meant boiling and scrubbing the second saucepan that the scrubber would be sterilised in. I looked at the knife, the chopping board, the teaspoon, the bowl. They were lined up like cannon fodder in a particularly nasty biological war. The cauliflower receded further and further into the distance as the things that needed to be cleaned stretched away on all sides like a hall of mirrors.

If you go by Annabel Karmel's *Feeding Your Baby and Toddler* book, tackling this next stage of your child's life requires a staggering amount of equipment, from processors and blenders to steamers and weaning bowls with heat-sensitive plastic spoons. Where she had a stainless steel, German-engineered, ergonomically designed, eco-friendly moulis-blender, I had an old tea-strainer. As I was detoxifying the tea-strainer, I managed to burn the cauliflower. I threw away the smoking saucepan and started again.

Two hours of hard work later, I had managed to produced two teaspoons of grey-white pulp. It looked as appetising as papier-maché.

Manoeuvring the baby into a feeding position was like cuddling mercury. By this time, I was so stressed and anxious, I could hardly tell which way was up. My heart was in my mouth as I put a tiny glop of pureé on the spoon and held it to his lips. Would he reject it? Would he lap it up? My whole fate seemed to hang in the balance. He loves me. He loves me not. His father, ever-more practical than I, shoved in the spoon. The baby slurped up the purée. I burst into tears.

I was ecstatic that he'd eaten something I'd cooked, crucifyingly embarassed that I'd fallen into the tender trap (cake = love) that any sensible feminist could have seen coming; and aghast that starting from now I'd have to do a repeat performance the next day, and the next, and the next...

Days followed days like fairground horses, each similar to the last, galloping, galloping and never catching up. There was no getting off the merry-go-round of shopping, washing, cooking, pulping, feeding and cleaning. As gardeners know as well as mothers, you can't grow a rose without shovelling shit, and as the solids grew more solid at one end, so they did at the other.

The kid never opened his mouth wide and happily. If his lips parted sufficiently to let out a sigh, I would slip in a spoon of gloop, scraping off the excess and reapplying it, like grouting a fiddly mosaic. And then hold my breath as he decided whether to swallow or spit. The mess was incredible. The amount of food around at the end of the meal seemed so much more than I'd started with, as though it had morphed and replicated like some alien life-form. As I beat back the rising tide of gunk, I send up a silent prayer of thanks to the God of Small half-Indian Things who had the foresight to arrange at least this part of our lives in a land without carpets.

Our attempts to get the baby to eat ranged from the gentle to the desperate. We would set out a bewildering variety of things before him: colourful things, stacking things, things with wheels and lights, things that jiggled and played tunes, anything to keep him from noticing us trying to get some food into his mouth. If sufficiently entranced, the part of his brain that regulated food intake would switch to auto-pilot and all would be well. Each mouthful swallowed made me giddy with delight. Each morsel rejected sent my spirits plummeting.

There is nothing quite so terrible as the cry of a hungry baby. It is the sound of the world unmaking itself. In the days following birth, women often feel as raw and tender as newborn beings themselves (I was prone to sit at bus stops sobbing copiously at the unfeeling speed of cars). A mew of hunger from your baby sounded like a piece of your own soul crying out in distress. The feeling of those post-partum days was not unlike religious conversion or surviving a natural disaster. I was head-over-heels in love, of course – but more than that, overwhelmed by a kind of world-encompassing, almost intergalactic, compassion. The thought that there existed at that very moment other babies who were hungry, was almost too much to bear. I believe this is not uncommon. But slowly, as I returned to 'normal' after the radical, human openness of birth, the psychological defenses came up, narrowing the love down somehow, focussing it like a beam, until I was again able to tolerate the intolerable, until other people's hungry children seemed merely irritating, inevitable and nothing to do with me.

His father and I would try to figure out some pattern to the baby's rudimentary tastes – he doesn't like carrot, it's too dry, it's too wet, mash it with dahi – but as far as I could see there was no logic to his preferences. One day he would love dal, the next spit it out. Dahi would be the in-thing for weeks, and then suddenly fall from favour. We were trapped in a labyrinth of shifting walls.

Witnessing our puny attempts to work our way out of the maze one day, a friend remarked, 'Oh, I'm sure he'll eat if he's hungry.' He might have been speaking Mandarin. The Mothership, of which I seemed to have become captain, was not powered by such logic. Our steering was set by a new constellation, our navigational tools intuition, hope and great, blind leaps of faith. Our fleet was innumerable, our experience almost nil, and our mission – to boldly go where hundreds and thousands of women have gone since time immemorial – seemed like the first such journey ever taken.

❈

As my life seemed to spin further and further out of control in a mad whirl of baby-centric duties, I turned to Gina Ford's *Contented Little Baby Book* for help. Like so many of the other baby books I'd seen, with their pristine tots and colour-coordinated cutlery, Ford's book bore little resemblance to my daily reality. There was, however, something oddly soothing about reading her meticulous instructions: 'He should be given the first breast at 5.30pm,

followed by the baby rice, then the second breast at 6.45pm
after the bath.' It was like spying on a laboratory experiment
involving white mice and tunnels.

Annabel Karmel's *Complete Cookbook for Babies and
Toddlers* was equally other-worldly. Filled with recipes to
make your mouth water, your pulse race and your heart
sink, her menus were not only nutritious and delicious, but
even *looked* like miniature art-works. For a six-month-old
baby, she suggested an evening dinner of fillet of cod with a
trio of vegetables. One cannot help but wonder if the baby
sent the wine back.

Looking at her perfectly-coiffed hair and her shiny-
clean children, I realised that Annabel was a creature from
a different dimension, where sculpting mashed potato into
garden snails or trimming cheese into heart-shapes are
considered perfectly normal activities for a busy young
mum. As we Earthlings all know, babies – like animals and
other simple organisms – 'feed' rather than eat. Look at a
baby closely and you can see that its toothless mouth is
better described as a 'mouthpart' or 'sucker'. Look at him
playing with his hands – those are more 'feelers' than
'fingers'. For a newborn child, the world is a kaleidoscopic
sensorium where touch and sound, taste and smell and
vision overlap. Gradually, as the different parts of the body
learn their specialisation, the senses move apart, becoming
distinct, refined, and focussed. Apart from all the practical
issues, to introduce concepts like 'starters', 'puddings' and
'side-dishes' into this poor mite's hitherto milky universe
seemed misguided to the point of perversity.

Surely there was some middle ground between Ford's

white-coated Übernanny on the one hand and Karmel's professional food stylist on the other? A small voice inside me said: look East, young woman – look around you. And sure enough, there were Indian women all around me, seeming to juggle the whole business of feeding and raising their offspring with consummate ease. I found it even embarrassing to talk about what a mess my life was in. It struck me that whilst the joint family system was flawed in many respects, it was pretty much perfect for bringing up children.

All my friends in England were either struggling to hold down jobs that would pay them enough to be able to afford childcare to be able to hold down the job or, alternatively, experiencing the sudden trauma of isolation, trapped at home looking after the baby while their partner worked. In India, similar bright, professional young women, got on with their bright professional lives while a whole stage crew of cleaners, cooks, helpers, servants, not to mention grandparents, uncles, aunts, and siblings took care of things at home. It seemed ideal – from the outside anyway – and their babies always seemed, well, if not *happier* then certainly plumper than mine. But I had seen enough of joint family life to know the turmoil and power struggles that are its very heartbeat, and although the palak paneer was almost certainly greener on that side of the fence, I wasn't ready to jump it yet.

❦

In the meantime, I was dashing to and from office, struggling to hold it all together, while everything seemed perilously

close to unravelling. I was constantly aware that my right
to have a professional career and not just be 'a wife and
mother', was a relatively recent phenomenon. Even one
generation back, such a choice was seen not as a right but
a privilege – and in the social strata below mine, not even
that, not even today. It's hardly surprising that many women
are reluctant to 'give up the day job' once they've had a
child. Looking after children, after all, is a low-status job. It
is 'woman's work' in the traditional sense of the phrase, and
to say that it's never done, is a vast understatement.

But what most people (and by that I mean 'non-
mothers' – male and female) don't realise is that the answer
to the problem is not more affordable childcare. Until
you're in it, until you *are* it, you cannot comprehend the
fundamental dilemma upon which motherhood is founded.
Novelist Rachel Cusk writes that 'birth is not merely that
which divides women from men: it also divides women
from themselves, so that a woman's understanding of what
it is to exist is profoundly changed… When she is with
[her children] she is not herself; when she is without them,
she is not herself; and so it is as difficult to leave your
children as it is to stay with them. To discover this is to feel
that your life has become irretrievably mired in conflict, or
caught in some mythic snare in which you will perpetually,
vainly struggle.'

A key part of feminist struggle has been to liberate women
from their household duties. A woman's place, I had grown
up to believe, is *not* in the kitchen. And yet, as more and more
of my waking hours revolved around exactly that room, I
realised that a straightforwardly feminist agenda, articulated

with what Cusk calls the 'blithe unsentimentality of the childless,' was no longer even available to me as an option. But how much more interesting, how much truer, how much more human to mumble through chaos rather than articulate with clarity, to acknowledge the contraditions, the pushmepullyou that powers the inner turbine of our lives. It seems that this is what 'second wave' feminism is so good at – not reducing the complexity, but opening to embrace it. Suddenly the condition of motherhood does not seem constraining and pitiable, a biological trap into which all but the stoutest-hearted feminists fall. It feels more like the embodiment of Derrida's notion of *différance* – the twin ruling gods of my life are deferral and repetition, after all. The divided, perpetually ensnared identity that Rachel Cusk describes seems to encompass not just the post-partum but the post-modern human condition.

❦

Eighteen months after the baby was born, I had achieved a slimline body that years of aerobics had failed to deliver. Despite the fact that my life seemed to revolve almost entirely around the issue of food, eating it myself never seemed to rank higher than 3 or 4 on my list of Things to Do. Then one day, I had to steady myself on the sink and fight off a bout of giddiness. Diagnosis – borderline malnutrition. Any nutrients that I'd managed to get into my body during the day were being syphoned off at night, as the baby breastfed his way through the dark hours. As the baby grew, I shrank. I had become a parable; a living cliché about women and their self-abnegation.

It was time to get a grip.

If giving birth was the first degree of separation, and introducing solids was the second, stopping breastfeeding was the third. It felt as though I were constructing a wall between us. I was terrified of holding the baby because then I would have to withhold myself from him. Desperate to comfort him with my presence, yet unable to come close to his flailing form for fear of driving him further into pitiable abstraction, searching for that which would not come. He cried as though the world were falling to pieces.

⁂

The world didn't fall to pieces. The centre held. And the beauty born was not terrible. It was rather sweet. With peachy cheeks.

Now, at two, I watch him drink from a cup; slurp up cereal with a spoon; nibble a rice-cake; chomp on a cob of sweetcorn – and I feel like I've conquered the world. We've made it, baby.

I'm no longer malnourished.

And you?

Well, you never were, my honeypot, my delectable morsel. Come here, so I can take a bite....

ANITA ROY was born in Calcutta in 1965, grew up in England, and has lived and worked in Delhi since 1995. She is senior editor with Zubaan, and runs their children's and young adults' imprint, Young Zubaan. Her non-fiction writing has appeared in several anthologies and she is a regular reviewer, critic and freelance writer. She edited the short story collection, *21 Under 40*, and is co-editor, with Urvashi Butalia, of the photography book, *Women Changing India*.

She is an avid and eclectic reader, an enthusiastic if erratic cyclist, a frustrated gardener, an aspiring novelist, and an ecological worrier, for whom motherhood came late, unplanned and deliciously in the form of her (now ten-year-old) son, Roshan.

Milky Ways
A Contemplation of the Hindi-movie Maa

JAI ARJUN SINGH

Around the age of 14, I took what was meant to be a temporary break from Hindi cinema, and ended up staying away for over a decade. Years of relishing masala movies may have resulted in a form of dyspepsia – there had been too many overwrought emotions, too much 'dhishoom dhishoom', too much of the strictly regimented quantities of Drama and Action and Tragedy and Romance and Comedy that existed in almost every mainstream Hindi film of the time. Besides, I had developed a love for Old Hollywood, which would become a gateway to world cinema, and satellite TV had started making it possible to indulge such interests.

One of my catalysts for escape was Alfred Hitchcock's *Psycho*, a film that is – among many other things – about a strange young man's special relationship with his equally strange mother. I won't bother with spoiler alerts for such a well-known pop-cultural artefact, so briefly: Norman Bates poisons his mom, preserves her body, walks around in her clothes and has conversations with himself in her voice. In his off-time, he murders young women as they shower.

None of this was a secret to me when I first saw the film, for a certain *Psycho* lore existed in my family. Years in advance, I had heard jokes about 'mummification' from my own mummy – apparently, in the early sixties, her school-going brother had returned from a movie-hall and informed their startled mother that he wished to keep her body in a sitting position in the living room after she passed on.

Hitchcock's film had a huge effect on the way I watched and thought about movies, but I must admit that my own relationship with my mother was squarer than Norman's. We quarrelled occasionally, but always in our own voices, and taxidermy did not obtrude upon our lives. Looking back, though, I think we could be described as unconventional in the context of the society we lived in. I was a single child, she was recently divorced, we had been through a lot together and were very close. But we were both – then, as now – private people, and so the relationship always respected personal space. We didn't spend much time on small talk, we tended to stay in our own rooms for large parts of the day (and this is how it remains, as I type these words in my shabby freelancer's 'office' in her flat). Yet I always shared the really important stuff with her, and I never thought this was unusual until I heard stories about all the things my friends – even the ones from the seemingly cool, cosmopolitan families – routinely hid from their parents: about girlfriends, or bunking college, or their first cigarette.

Some of this may help explain why I was feeling detached from the emotional excesses of Hindi cinema in my early teens. In his book on *Deewaar*, the historian Vinay Lal notes,

'No more important or poignant relationship exists in Indian society than that between mother and son, and the Hindi film best exemplifies the significance of this nexus.' This may be so, but I can say with my hand on my heart (or 'mother-swear', if you prefer) that even at age 14, I found little to relate to in Hindi-film depictions of mothers.

Can you blame me though? Here, off the top of my head (and with only some basic research to confirm that I hadn't dreamt up these wondrous things), are some of my movie memories from around the time I left the temple of Hindi cinema:

- In the remarkably bad *Jamai Raja*, Hema Malini is a wealthy tyrant who makes life difficult for her son-in-law. Some of this is played for comedy, but the film clearly disapproves of the idea of a woman as the head of the house. (Even a better film from a decade earlier, Hrishikesh Mukherjee's *Khubsoorat*, couldn't resist caricaturing the matriarch who wields an iron hand over husband and sons.) Cosmic balance is restored only when the saas gets her comeuppance and asks the damaad's forgiveness. Of course, he graciously clasps her joint hands and asks her not to embarrass him; that's the hero's privilege.
- In *Sanjog*, when she loses the little boy she had thought of as a son, Jaya Prada glides about in a white sari, holding a piece of wood wrapped in cloth and singing a song with the refrain 'Zoo zoo zoo zoo zoo'. This song still plays incessantly in one of the darker rooms of my memory palace; I shudder whenever I recall the tune.
- In *Aulad*, the ubiquitous Jaya Prada is a woman named

Yashoda who battles another woman (named, what else, Devaki) for custody of the bawling Baby Guddu, while obligatory Y-chromosome Jeetendra stands around looking smug and noble at the same time.

- In her short-lived comeback in *Aandhiyan*, a middle-aged Mumtaz dances with her screen son in a cringe-inducingly affected display of parental hipness. 'Mother and son made a lovely love feeling with their dance and song (sic),' goes a comment on the YouTube video of the song '*Duniya Mein Tere Siva*'. Also: 'I like the perfect matching mother and son love chemistry behind the song, it is a eternal blood equation (sic).' The quality of these comments is indistinguishable from the quality of the film they extol.

- And in *Doodh ka Karz*, a woman breastfeeding her child is so moved by the sight of a hungry cobra nearby that she squeezes a few drops of milk out and puts it in a bowl for him. The snake looks disgusted but sips some of the milk anyway. Naturally, this incident becomes the metaphorical umbilical cord that attaches him to this new 'maa' for life.

As one dire memory begets another, the title of that last film reminds me that two words were in common currency in the eighties' Hindi cinema: '*doodh*' and '*khoon*'. Milk and blood. Since these twin fluids were central to every hyper-dramatic narrative about family honour and revenge, our movie halls (or video rooms, since few sensible people I knew spent money on theatre tickets at the time) resounded with some mix of the following proclamations:

'Maa ka doodh piya hai toh baahar nikal!' ('If you have drunk your mother's milk, come out!')

'Yeh tumhara apna khoon hai.' ('He is your own blood.')

'Main tera khoon pee jaaoonga.' ('I will drink your blood.')

Both liquids were treated as equally nourishing; both were, in different ways, symbols of the hero's vitality. I have no recollection of the two words being used together in a sentence, but it would not amaze me to come across a scene from an eighties relic where the hero says: *'Kuttay! Maine apni maa ka doodh piya hai. Ab tera khoon piyoonga.'* ('Dog! I have drunk my mother's milk, now I will drink your blood.') It would suggest a rite of passage consistent with our expectations of the über-macho lead: as a child you drink mother's milk, but you're all grown up now and bad man's blood is more intoxicating than fake Johnnie Walker.

Narcissists, angry young men and deadly guitars

All this is a complicated way of saying that I do not, broadly speaking, hold the eighties in high esteem any more. But that decade is a soft target. Casting the net much wider, here's a proposal: mainstream Hindi cinema has never had a sustained tradition of interesting mothers.

This is, of course, a generalisation; there have been exceptions in major films. Looming over every larger-than-life mother portrayal is *Mother India,* which invented (or at least highlighted) many of the things we think of as clichés today: the mother as metaphor for nation/land/nourishing source; the mother as righteous avenging angel, ready to shred her own heart and shoot her wayward son if it is for the Greater Good. Despite the self-conscious weightiness of this film's narrative, it is possible to see its central character, Radha, as an individual first and only then as a symbol – which is probably a credit to Nargis's performance more than anything else.

But a basic problem is that for much of her history, the Hindi-film mother has been a cipher – someone with no real personality of her own, existing mainly as the prism through which we view the male lead. Much like the sister whose function was to be raped and to commit suicide in a certain type of movie, the mother was a pretext for the playing out of the hero's emotions and actions.

Anyone well acquainted with Hindi cinema knows that one of its dominant personalities has been the narcissistic leading man. (Note: the films themselves don't intend him to be seen thus.) This quality is usually linked to the persona of the star-actor playing the role, and so it can take many forms: the jolly hero/tragic hero/romantic hero/anti-hero who ambles, trudges or swaggers through the world knowing full well that he is its centre of attention. (Presumably he never grew out of the '*maa ka laadla*' mould.) So here is Raj Kapoor's little tramp smiling bravely through his hardships, and here is the studied tragic grandiosity of Dilip Kumar, and here is Dev Anand's splendid conceit (visible in all the films he made from the mid-sixties on) that every woman from age 15 upwards wants only to fall into his arms. In later decades, this narcissism would be manifest in the leading man as the vigilante superhero.

A 'maa' can easily become a foil for such personalities –

our film history is dotted with sympathetic but ineffectual mothers. Though often played by accomplished character actors such as Achala Sachdev and Leela Mishra, these women were rarely central to the movies in question. If you have only a dim memory of Guru Dutt's *Pyaasa*, for example, you might forget that the self-pitying poet (one of the most doggedly masochistic heroes in our cinema) has a mother too – she is a marginalised figure, watching with some perplexity as he wanders the streets waiting for life to deal him its next blow. And her death adds to the garland of sorrows that he so willingly carries around his neck.

While Dutt made a career out of not smiling, the protagonist of Raj Kapoor's bloated *Mera Naam Joker* earned his livelihood by making people laugh. Essentially, however, Raju the clown is as much of a sympathy-seeker as the poet in the gutter is. *Mera Naam Joker* includes a magnificently maudlin scene where the joker continues with his act ('The show must go on!' growls circus-master Dharmendra) just a few minutes after learning that his mother has died. As he smiles heroically through his pain, his friends watching backstage wipe their tears – cues for the film's viewer to do the same.

Speaking of Raj Kapoor, I often wonder what impression Russian movie-watchers must have of Indian men and their mother fetishes. If Kapoor was the most popular Hindi-film star in the former Soviet Union, an improbable second was Mithun Chakraborty, the stature of whose 1982 film *Disco Dancer* in that part of the world is among the profoundest cinematic mysteries. (Possibly apocryphal stories are still told about how Indian visitors to the USSR in the Iron

Curtain days could clear borders by warbling 'Jimmy Jimmy' whereupon stern guards would drop their rifles and wave them through.)

Among *Disco Dancer*'s many pleasures is the most thrilling mother-related dialogue in a Hindi film. Even today, I would walk many a harsh mile to hear the following words echoing through a movie hall: *'Issko guitar phobia ho gaya hai. Guitar ne isske maa ko maara.'* ('He has developed guitar phobia. A guitar killed his mother.')

This demands some elucidation. Jimmy (Mithun) has become so popular that his disco-dancing rivals scheme to electrocute him with a 5000-volt current. But his widowed maa, having just finished her daily puja for his continued health and success, learns about this fiendish saazish. She reaches the venue in time to grab the tampered guitar before Jimmy does, which results in the most electrifying death scene of a Hindi-movie mother you'll ever see.

The subtext to this surreal moment is that the hero is emasculated by the removal of his mother. As one inadvertently Oedipal plot synopsis I have read puts it, 'After his mother's death Jimmy finds himself unable to perform. Will he be able to recover from the tragedy and start performing again?' (Note the contrast with *Mera Naam Joker's* Raju, who does indeed 'perform' just a few seconds after his loss – but no one doubts that he is now a hollow shell of a person.)

As these scenes and countless others indicate, Hindi cinema loves dead moms. In the same year as *Disco Dancer*, there was an overhyped 'acting battle' between Dilip Kumar and Amitabh Bachchan in *Shakti*. It played out through the film, but never as intensely as in the scene where the mutinous son tries to reach out to his policeman dad in the room where the dead body of Sheetal (wife and mother to the two men) lies. In the context of the narrative, the mother's corpse becomes the final frontier for a clash of ideologies and life experiences.

❦

I'm surprised at how long it has taken me to arrive at Amitabh Bachchan, given that all my early movie-watching centred on him – and also given that no other major Hindi-film personality has been as strongly associated with filial relationships. But perhaps I've been trying to repress a memory. One of the last things I saw before forsaking Bollywood in 1991 was this scene from the fantasy film *Ajooba*. Bachchan (make-up doing little to conceal that he was playing a character half his age) brings an old woman to the seaside where a dolphin is splashing about, beaming and making the sounds that dolphins will. With sonly fondness in his eyes and a scant regard for taxonomical accuracy, AB says: *'Yeh machli meri maa hai.'* ('This fish is my mother.')

This could be a version of post-modern irony, for Bachchan had come a long way from the star-making films in which he played son to the long-suffering Nirupa Roy. Unlike the 'mother' in *Ajooba*, Roy was a land mammal, but she seemed always to have a personal lake of tears to splash about in at short notice.

Was that too irreverent? (Am I failing the test of the good Indian boy whose eyes must lower at the very mention of 'maa'?) Well, respect should ideally be earned. The mothers played by Roy are good examples of the ciphers I mentioned earlier, and though she often got substantial screen time, I don't think it was put to much good use.

Consider an early scene in Prakash Mehra's *Muqaddar ka Sikander*. When the orphan Sikander recovers Roy's stolen purse for her, she expresses a wish to be his new mother: *'Beta, ab se main tumhari maa hoon.'* *'Sach, maa? Tum bahut achi ho, maa,'* ('Really, mother? You are very nice, mother') he replies. Having rushed through these lines, they then exit the frame together in the jerky fast-forward style of the silent era's Keystone Kops. There is a reason for the haste: the audience wants to see the adult Sikander (Bachchan), so the preamble must be dispensed with. But the result is the trivialising of an important relationship – we are simply 'told' that they are now mother and son, and that's that. It's a good example of character development scrubbing the shoes of the star system.

Manmohan Desai's *Amar Akbar Anthony* is another movie very dear to my heart (and a genuine classic of popular storytelling), but it would be a stretch to claim that Roy's Bharati (you know, the woman who simultaneously receives blood from her three grown-up sons) is a fleshed-out person. Medically speaking, she scarcely appears human at all: in the first minutes of the film we learn that Bharati is suffering from life-threatening tuberculosis; a while later, she carelessly loses her eyesight and the TB is never again mentioned; years pass and here she is, distributing flowers, haphazardly stumbling in and out of the lives of the three heroes; eventually her sight is restored by a Sai Baba statue.

But it is well-nigh impossible to write about Bachchan and his mothers without reference to Yash Chopra's *Deewaar* (and to an extent, the same director's *Trishul*). *Deewaar* is to Hindi cinema what the James Cagney-starrer *White Heat* ('Made it, Ma! Top of the world!') was to Hollywood: the most quoted and parodied of all mother-son movies. In no small part this is because the film was a fulcrum for one of our most iconic movie personalities, the angry young man Vijay.

Speaking for myself, childhood memory and countless spoofs on music channels had turned *Deewaar* into a montage of famous images and dialogues: Bachchan brooding outside the temple; a dramatic pealing of bells and a prolonged death scene; Shashi Kapoor bleating '*Bhai*' and, with nostrils flaring self-righteously, the famous line '*Mere paas Maa hai.*' But when I saw it as an adult, I was surprised by how powerful the film still was, and how its most effective scenes were the quieter ones. One scene that sticks with me is when the mother – Sumitra Devi – is unwell and the fugitive Vijay can't see her because police have been posted around the hospital. He waits in a van while his girlfriend goes to check on the level of security. She returns, tells him things aren't looking good; and Vijay (who is wearing dark glasses – a chilling touch in this night-time scene) says in a deadpan voice, his face a blank slate, '*Aur main apne maa tak nahin pahunch sakta hoon.*' ('And I can't even reach my mother.') There is no overt attempt at pathos or irony (how many other Indian actors of the time would have played the scene this way?), just the stoicism of a man who knows that the walls are closing in.

In another scene Vijay hesitantly calls his mother on the phone, arranges to meet her at the temple, then tries to say something more but can't get the words out and puts the receiver down instead. The film's power draws as much from these discerning beats of silence as from its flaming Salim-Javed dialogue. However, little of that power comes directly from the mother's character. Sumitra Devi is defined by her two sons, and to my eyes at least, there is something perfunctory and insipid even about the moral strength she shows.

There is a tendency, when we assess Hindi cinema, to make sweeping statements about similar types of movies. Frequently, I hear that *Deewaar* and *Trishul* are the same film because both are built around the theme of a son trying to erase his mother's sufferings by rising in the world – even literally, by signing deed papers for new skyscrapers, the constructions she once worked on as a labourer (Vijay, like James Cagney, is trying to make it to 'the top'). But there are key differences in the central character's motivations in the two movies, and I would argue that *Deewaar* is the superior film overall because it is more tightly constructed.

However, *Trishul* scores in one important regard: it is one of the few Bachchan films where the mother has a personality. Cynically speaking, this could be because she dies early in the film and isn't required to hold the stage for three hours, but I think it has a lot to do with the performance of Waheeda Rehman – an actress who made a career of illuminating mediocre movies with her presence.

'*Tu mere saath rahega munne,*' sings this mother, who has been abandoned by her lover – the song will echo through the movie and fuel her son's actions. *'Main tujhe rehem ke saaye mein na palne doongi'* ('I will not raise you under the shade of sympathy'), she tells her little boy as she lets him toil alongside her,*'Zindagani ki kadi dhoop mein jalne doongi / Taake tap tap ke tu faulad bane / maa ki audlad bane.'* She wants him to burn in the sun so he becomes as hard as steel. He has to earn his credentials if he wants the right to be called her son.

With a lesser performer in the role, this could have been hackneyed stuff (in any case the basic premise is at least as old as Raj Kapoor's *Awaara*), but Rehman makes it dignified and compelling, giving it a psychological dimension that is lacking in all those Nirupa Roy roles. It's a reminder that an excellent performer can, to some extent at least, redeem an unremarkable part. (I would make a similar case for Durga Khote in *Mughal-e-Azam*, which – on paper at least – was a film about two imperial male egos in opposition.)

Motherly vignettes (and an absence)

In discussing these films, I've probably revealed my ambivalence towards popular Hindi cinema. One problem for someone who tries to engage with these films is that even the best of them tend to be disjointed; a critic is required to approach a movie as a collection of parts rather than as a unified whole. Perhaps it would be fair then to admit that there have been certain 'mother moments' that worked for me on their own terms, independently of the overall quality of the films.

One of them occurred in – of all things – a Manoj Kumar film. Kumar was famous for his motherland-obsession, demonstrated in a series of 'patriotic' films that often exploited their heroines. (See Hema Malini writhing in the rain in *Kranti*, or Saira Banu in *Purab aur Paschim*, subject to the controlling male gaze that insists a woman must be covered up – after the hero and the audience has had a good eyeful, of course.) But one of his rare non-patriotism-themed films contains a weirdly compelling representation of the mother-as-an-absent-presence. The film is the 1972 *Shor*, about a boy so traumatised by his mother's death that he loses the power of speech, and the song is the plaintive Laxmikant-Pyarelal composition '*Ek Pyaar ka Nagma Hai*'.

In too many Hindi movies of that time, ethereal music is played out to banal images, but this sequence makes at least a theoretical nod to creativity. The visuals take the shape of a shared dream-memory involving the father, the little boy and the mother when she was alive; the setting is a beach and the composite elements include a violin, a drifting, symbolism-laden bunch of balloons, and Nanda. Mirror imagery is used: almost every time we see the mother or the boy, we also see their blurred reflections occupying half the screen; occasionally, the lens focus is tinkered with to make both images merge into each other or disappear altogether. Even though the setting is ostensibly a happy and 'realist' one, Nanda is thus rendered a distant, ghostly figure.

I'm not saying this is done with any sophistication – it is at best an ambitious concept, shoddily executed; you can sense the director and cinematographer constrained by the available technology. But the basic idea does come through: what we are seeing is a merging of past and present, and the dislocation felt by a child whose mother has abruptly been taken from him.

[While on absent mothers, a quick aside on *Sholay*. Ramesh Sippy's iconic film was heavily inspired by the look of the American and Italian Westerns, but it also deviated from the Hindi-film idiom in one significant way: in the absence of a mother-child relationship. The only real mother figure in the story, Basanti's sceptical maasi, becomes a target of mirth in one of the film's drollest scenes. Most notably, the two leads Veeru and Jai (played by Dharmendra and Bachchan) are orphans who have only ever had each other. We tend to take *Sholay* for granted today, but it's surprising, when you think about it, that the leading men of a Hindi movie of the time should so summarily lack any maternal figure, real or adopted.]

In Vijay Anand's thriller *Jewel Thief*, a clever deception is perpetrated on the viewer. Early on, Vinay (Dev Anand) is told that Shalu (Vyjayantimala) is pining because she has been abandoned by her fiancé. This provides a set-up for the song '*Rula ke Gaya Sapna Mera*', where Vinay hears Shalu singing late at night; we see her dressed in white, weeping quietly; the lyrics mourn her loss; our expectations from seeing Dev Anand and Vyjayantimala together in this romantic setting lead us to assume that what is being lamented is a broken love affair. But later, we learn that though Shalu's tears were genuine, she was really crying for a little boy who has been kidnapped (this is, strictly speaking, her much younger brother, but the relationship is closer to that of a mother and son, and the song was an expression if it). It's a rare example of a Hindi-movie song sequence being used to mislead, and changing its meaning when you revisit it.

There is also a lovely little scene in a non-mainstream Hindi film, Sudhir Mishra's *Dharavi*. Cab-driver Rajkaran, his wife and little son are struggling to make ends meet as one mishap follows another. Rajkaran's old mother has come to visit them in the city and one night, after a series of events that leaves the family bone-tired and mentally exhausted, there is a brief shot of two pairs of sons and mothers, with the former curled up with their heads in the latter's laps – the grown-up Rajkaran is in the same near-foetal pose as his little boy. It's the sort of image that captures a relationship more eloquently than pages of over-expository script.

Breaking the weepie mould: new directions

One of the funniest mothers in a Hindi film was someone who appeared only in a photograph – the madcap 1962 comedy *Half Ticket* has a scene where the protagonist Vijay (no relation to the Angry Young Man) speaks to a picture of his tuberculosis-afflicted mother. TB-afflicted mothers are usually no laughing matter in Hindi cinema, but this is a Kishore Kumar film, and thus it is that a close-up of the mother's photo reveals… Kishore Kumar in drag. This could be a little nod to Alec Guinness and Peter Sellers playing women in Ealing Studio comedies of the fifties, or it could be a case of prefiguring (since the story will hinge on Kumar posing as a child). Either way, it is a rare instance in old cinema of a mother being treated with light-hearted irreverence.

But as mentioned earlier, the more characteristic mother treatment has been one of deification – which, ironically, results in diminishment. When the maternal figure is put on a pedestal, you don't see her as someone with flaws, whimsies, or heaven forbid, an interior life. (One of Indian cinema's starkest treatments of this theme was in Satyajit Ray's 1960 film *Devi*, with the 14-year-old Sharmila Tagore as a bride whose world turns upside down when her childlike father-in-law proclaims her a reincarnation of the Mother Goddess.) And so, if there has been a shift in mother portrayals in recent times, it has hinged on a willingness to humanise.

Around the late eighties, a certain sort of 'liberal' movie mum had come into being. I remember nodding in appreciation at the scene in *Maine Pyaar Kiya* where Prem (Salman Khan) discusses prospective girlfriends with his mom (played by the always-likeable Reema Lagoo). Still, when it came to the crunch, you wouldn't expect these seemingly broad-minded women to do anything that would seriously shake the patriarchial tradition. In her younger days Farida Jalal was among the feistiest of the actresses who somehow never became A-grade stars, but by the time she played Kajol's mother in *Dilwale Dulhaniya le Jaayenge*, she had settled into the role of the woman who can feel for young love – and be a friend and confidant to her daughter – while also knowing, through personal experience, that women in her social setup 'don't even have the right to make promises'. The two young lovers in this film can be united only when the heart of the stern father melts.

Such representations – mothers as upholders of 'traditional values', even when those values are detrimental to the interests of women – are not going away any time soon (see Jaya Bachchan in *Kabhi Khushi Kabhi Gham*), and why would they, if cinema is to be a part-mirror to society? An amusing motif in the 2011 film *No One Killed Jessica* was a middle-aged mother as a figure hiding behind the curtain (literally 'in pardah'), listening to the men's conversations and speaking up only to petulantly demand the return of her son (who is on the lam, having cold-bloodedly murdered a young woman). It seems caricatured at first, but when you remember the details of the real-life Jessica Lal–Manu Sharma case that the film is based on, there is nothing surprising about it.

But it is also true that in the multiplex era of the last decade, mother representations – especially in films with urban settings – have been more varied than they were in the past. (Would it be going too far to say 'truer to life'? I do feel that the best contemporary Hindi films are shaped by directors and screenwriters who know their milieus and characters very well, and have a greater willingness to tackle individual complexity than many of their predecessors did.)

Thus, *Jaane Tu...Ya Jaane Na* featured a terrific performance by Ratna Pathak Shah as Savitri Rathore, a wisecracking mom whose banter with her dead husband's wall-portrait marks a 180-degree twist on every maudlin wall-portrait scene from movies of an earlier time. (Remember the weepy monologues that went '*Munna ab BA Pass ho gaya hai. Aaj agar aap hamaare saath hote, aap itne khush hote*'?) One gets the sense that unlike her mythological namesake, this Savitri is relieved that she no longer has to put up with her husband's three-dimensional presence! Then there is the Kirron Kher character in *Dostana*, much more orthodox to begin with: a jokily over-the-top song sequence, '*Maa da laadla bigad gaya*', portrays her dismay about the possibility that her son is homosexual, and she is even shown performing witchery to 'cure' him. But she does eventually come around, gifting bangles to her 'daughter-in-law' and wondering if traditional Indian rituals might accommodate something as alien as gay marriage. These scenes are played for laughs (and in any case, the son isn't *really* gay), but they do briefly touch on very real cultural conflicts and on the ways in which parents from conservative backgrounds often have to change to keep up with the times.

With the aid of nuanced scripts, thoughtful casting and good performances, other small bridges have been crossed in recent years. *Taare Zameen Par* – the story of a dyslexic child – contains an uncontrived depiction of the emotional bond between mother and child (as well as the beautiful song '*Maa*'). At age 64, Bachchan acquired one of his most entertaining screen moms, the then 94-year-old Zohra Segal, in R. Balki's *Cheeni Kum*. A few years after that, the somewhat gimmicky decision to cast him as a Progeria-afflicted child in *Paa* meant he could play son to Vidya Balan, who was less than half his age. There is quiet dignity in this portrayal of a single working mother, though the film did kowtow to tradition (and to the ideal of the romantic couple) by ensuring that she is reunited with her former lover at the end.

One of the last Hindi films I saw before writing this piece – another Balan-starrer, the thriller *Kahaani* – has as its protagonist a heavily pregnant woman alone in the city, searching for her missing husband. This makes for an interesting psychological study because the quality of the film's suspense (and the effect of the twist in its tail) depends on our accumulating feelings – sympathy, admiration – for this mother-to-be, laced with the mild suspicion that we mustn't take everything about her at face value. I wasn't surprised to discover that some people felt a little betrayed (read: emotionally manipulated) by the ending, which reveals that Vidya Bagchi wasn't pregnant after all – the revelation flies in the face of everything Hindi cinema has taught us about the sanctity of motherhood.

※

Given Vinay Lal's observation about the centrality of the mother-son relationship in Indian society, it is perhaps inevitable that our films have a much more slender tradition of 'mother-daughter' relationships. Going by all the gossip over the decades about dominating moms accompanying their starlet daughters to movie sets, the real-life stories may have been spicier than anything depicted on screen. And in fact, one of the scariest scenes from any Hindi film of the last decade involves just such a portrayal.

It occurs in Zoya Akhtar's excellent *Luck by Chance*, a self-reflective commentary on the nature of stardom in Hindi cinema. The young rose Nikki Walia (Isha Sharvani) is doing one of those cutesy photo shoot-cum-interviews that entail completing sentences like 'My favourite colour is _____.' At one point her mother Neena (Dimple Kapadia in an outstanding late-career performance), a former movie star herself, barges into the room and peremptorily begins giving instructions. We see Nikki's expression (we have already noted how cowered she is by her mother's presence) and feel a little sorry for her. 'Neena-ji, can we have a photo of both of you?' the reporter asks. Neena-ji looks flattered but says no, she isn't in a state fit to be photographed – why don't you shoot Nikki against that wall, she says, pointing somewhere off-screen, and then sashaying off.

A few seconds later the shoot continues. 'Your favourite person _____?' Nikki is asked. We get a full shot of the wall behind her – it is covered end to end with a colossal photo of Neena from her early days. 'My mother,' Nikki replies mechanically.

The younger Kapadia in that photo is breathtakingly beautiful, but as a depiction of a child swallowed up by a parent's personality, this brief shot is just as terrifying to my eyes as the closing scene of *Psycho*, with Norman Bates staring out at the camera, speaking to us in his mother's voice – for all practical purposes, back in the womb. *Luck by Chance* contains other scenes suggesting that the predatorial Neena is bent on putting her daughter through everything she herself had experienced in the big bad industry. Do these scenes get additional power from the viewer's non-diagetic knowledge that in real life, Dimple Kapadia herself entered the film industry at a disturbingly early age? You decide. Still, with the history of mainstream Hindi cinema being what it is, we should be grateful for this newfound variety, for stronger character development, and for at least *some* maternal representations that aren't drenched in sentimentalism.

We've always had the noble, self-sacrificing and marginalised mothers and we'll continue to have them – in cinema, as in life. So here's to a few more of the other sorts: more Neena-jis, more sardonic Savitris, a few moms like the hard-drinking salon-owner in *Vicky Donor*, not-really-mothers like Vidya Bagchi – and even, if it ever comes to that, a desi Mrs Bates staring unblinkingly from her chair, asking her son to please go to the kitchen and make her some chai instead of ogling at chaalu young women through the peephole.

JAI ARJUN SINGH is a Delhi-based writer and critic. He has edited the anthology *The Popcorn Essayists: What Movies do to Writers*, authored a book about the 1983 film *Jaane bhi do Yaaro*, and written for such publications as *Business Standard*, *The Hindustan Times*, Yahoo, *Tehelka*, *The Caravan*, *The Sunday Guardian*, *The Hindu* and *Forbes India*. In the bloated archives of his culture blog Jabberwock (http://jaiarjun. blogspot.in) you will find his writings about cinema and literature, as well as stray thoughts on tennis, parents-in-law, nasty water tanks, exploding letter-boxes, Ekta Kapoor serials and many other subjects. Despite being saddled with a Y-chromosome, Jai got to mother a very special canine child named Foxie for four years, and it was the most meaningful and enriching experience of his life. She departed, leaving an immeasurably big hole, just a few days after this essay was finished; it's dedicated to her.

The Devi Makers

KISHWAR DESAI

Eighteen-year-old Sarita's new home looked very unlike her old one, but in some ways it was exactly the same. Her old home after all, had been an orphanage and she had never been allowed to forget the circumstances under which she had been taken into care, just after her birth.

From when she was old enough to understand, the old dayen – the witch who ran the institution – had told her over and over again, that her mother was a characterless woman, who had lived in the household of the local politician.

'It was a toofani raat,' the dayen would say dramatically. 'When your mother came with you in her arms and fell at my feet. While the wind screamed and wailed outside, she begged me to take you in. But I refused, saying that the Saraswati Devi Anaath Ashram is only for the children of the unfortunate. Not for those who were trying to get rid of their sins. And slammed the door in her face.'

How the dayen made the distinction between acceptable and unacceptable children was difficult to fathom because no baby came with a character certificate imprinted on her forehead.

'But I always know... I know when a fallen woman

comes to me for help. And I know when a baby is born under *those* circumstances.' The dayen would pause at this critical juncture and her eyes would roll and glow with remembered warmth. 'And then the MLA sahib called. Himself!' she would cackle – her soft, plump hands running through her well-oiled hair as she shook it free from the bun, the hairpin clenched between her teeth.

'Take the baby, he said. I will make it up to you. And so …'. There would be another pause as she would swiftly twist her hair into a rope and then roll it up. The denouement came as she wrenched the pin from her teeth and stuck it firmly into the jooda.

'And so… I took *you* in. Haramzaadi.' Bastard child.

For a long time Sarita believed that her name was Haraamzaadi. And she would introduce herself to strangers who visited the orphanage with that name. It never failed to make everyone laugh. But many would-be parents backed away in horror. When she was four she finally understood why – because now the dayen would slap her and tell her not to use foul words.

'Sarita is your name, bewakoof! Say that after me!'

'Sarita is my name, bewakoof,' Sarita would repeat. And that made everyone laugh even more.

But that laughter chilled her as she grew up and more and more children left the orphanage – but no one seemed to want her. She became adept at looking after the dayen and her needs. And it was obvious that the dayen was pleased no one had adopted her. Because, thus, her access to the MLA and her job was sealed in perpetuity. Sarita was lucky for her.

So to all prospective parents who were drawn to the pale, pretty child, she would point out all of Sarita's failings, which of course changed as she grew up. At every age she had a new complaint.

'She is too thin, doesn't eat very well,' the dayen would proclaim sorrowfully, hinting at future problems. That was when Sarita was eight and a couple from Canada came looking for a child to adopt. They were keen on an older girl so they could give her a fresh start of life. But at every visit they were told about a litany of psychological issues that Sarita seemed to have developed. From rebelliousness to bed wetting. Everything. Finally, to the dayen's relief, they settled for someone else.

Sarita longed to tell the Canadians how much she had enjoyed the toys they had brought for her – and that the dayen had taken them away to give to other children. She also wanted to tell them that she had never wet her bed in her life. Ever.

However, the dayen made sure she wasn't alone with them at any point, and Sarita knew all about silences by then. There was no point speaking up because that would only make the dayen angry. And since she was the only one who seemed to want Sarita, and was very possessive about her, Sarita didn't want to create an issue over anything. She had learnt to be obedient and keep her thoughts to herself.

Sarita was not allowed to go out of the orphanage. It was run by a private trust for abandoned girls and the outside world also had limited access to it, and so they were more or less safe inside. Unlike other orphanages run by the government there were few scandals, for which the warden took complete credit.

Sometimes the dayen boasted how much money she had been offered for selling the girls into prostitution. And she told Sarita and the other girls, in graphic detail, what would happen to them if they tried to run away. She said this basically so that they did not get any fancy ideas about jumping the walls.

The warden insisted that her primary aim was to make her girls into 'devis' – and she prayed everyday that they would be free of sin and all the allurements of the flesh. It is a vice, she said. And women are more vulnerable because they get trapped. And the worst thing they could do was have another girl child. What a terrible fate, there would be no nirvana!

'Better to be like me,' she told Sarita. 'Remain unmarried, a virgin and pure. Not like your mother, that daughter of a haramzaadi. And then on top of that she had a girl child, sin upon sin upon sin… impossible to wipe out in a thousand births… taubah, taubah.' The dayen then spat paan into a bowl under the bed. Among Sarita's many tasks was also to empty out the container once a day.

She began to wonder if she was actually becoming a 'devi' of some kind, because now she was the oldest girl in the orphanage. Though she had little knowledge of her own beauty, she knew that she must have something special about her because outsiders began to look at her rather more closely when she passed by. Perhaps it was her long black hair, or the colour of her skin, or the way her eyes were shaped, and their strange blue colour. She had no idea what it was but everyone seemed to notice her now that she was eighteen years old. The dayen saw the attention Sarita was attracting and grew increasingly unhappy about it. She would pointedly shoo her away when there were visitors. And, of course, since she was just another inmate of the Saraswati Devi Anaath Ashram, why would anyone really bother with her?

The issue blew up one day when the MLA was visiting and asked to see her. He had heard that she had grown up into a lovely young girl. Clucking and grumbling, the dayen forced her into a shabby black salwar suit and oiled her hair so that she looked a little less pretty perhaps. But the MLA, a plump, rosy-cheeked man with a sharp-edged moustache, seemed delighted to see her.

'I think we should get her married. She seems healthy – will make a good wife for someone,' he said, while his lackeys nodded eagerly. Weddings, even those of penniless orphans, always meant money for everyone. Besides, this time the MLA would generous, as everyone knew he had a connection to this girl.

Sarita's heart pounded with fear. What would this do to her future 'devi' status that the dayen said she should aspire to? And what if, after her wedding, she had a baby girl? It didn't seem like a good idea at all.

She looked at the MLA with trepidation, but as usual was unable to break her silence. Either to protest or to accuse him of anything. She remembered what had happened to her mother, probably under this cheerful man's guidance.

Her mother had disappeared after that 'toofani raat'. Some days later a woman's body had surfaced in the well.

And Sarita often thought of her mother like that. An open haired woman with blue eyes like hers floating in the shallow well water, staring up at the sky. Perhaps she had remembered her daughter at least once before she jumped or was forced to jump. Villagers stopped drinking water from the well, after she was found there.

But then, a miracle occurred and they didn't need the well anymore. Oddly enough, after her death, ground water began to rise, and crops began to flourish. Years of drought mysteriously disappeared and all taps began to flow with sweet water. People from surrounding villages flocked to drink the water from their village.

It was all attributed to the woman in the well. She had been a devi!

Soon a temple was built in her memory. But, in deference to the MLA, it was not named after Sarita's mother. It was given a more generic name, the Devi Mata Mandir. This way no one would be blamed for the woman's death and she would not be identified. But the deity in the mandir had long black hair and blue-green eyes, and floated in a shallow pool.

And now the MLA had come to send Sarita away too. But as always, she kept quiet.

A few weeks later, in a public ceremony organised by the MLA and attended by many state ministers, six of the orphanage's older girls were married to six chosen boys in a widely televised event. The orphanage had advertised for eligible men and since there was a severe shortage of girls in the state, a surprising number of young men had applied. Finally the selection of the boys became a national event, broadcast live, as the MLA chose the names of the six lucky men in an open lottery. Other states, where the percentage of girls was also declining, were urged to follow the shining example of this semi-rural area near Agra. None of the chosen grooms were rich and no dowry was given, except in Sarita's case (the dowry was handed over secretly).

And now Sarita was in her new home, which was similar in some ways to the 'home' she had left behind. Though she could no longer lead an isolated life here.

Just as she had looked after the needs of the dayen, she now had to look after her husband, Kishen, as well as his parents all day, and queue up for the municipal water at 4 am. along with other women in the locality, as well. She also had to get used to city life. For the first time she was out on the streets like a normal woman. The traffic sounds and all the raucousness and aggression made it tough for her to settle down immediately. She sometimes longed to be back with the dayen and the dull but strict routine of the orphanage as her mother-in-law's grumbling could be more abrasive than that of the dayen. It seems she had only exchanged one witch for another. She was on her feet all day till late at night.

And once she fell pregnant, a new set of worries began to haunt her. Her fears did not allow her to confide in anyone at her new home. She did not even tell Kishen, who had turned out to be a gentle and kind man. He looked after her very well, in his own silent fashion, surprising her by buying small gifts of flowers and sweets and even taking her out, once in a while, to see a film. She hadn't thought anyone would be so good to her, and now she was devastated at the thought that her body might betray her and give him a girl child. Her mother-in-law had announced many times that she wanted a grandson and that is why they had agreed to marry their son off to a girl who brought no dowry. She never referred to the fact that the MLA had 'donated' 71,000 rupees to the family for their son, a painter of film hoardings, to marry her.

Kishen's work wasn't going too well, now that computers were used for designing film posters, and so they would often discuss how a grandson at least would bring joy to the family. And give them hope for the future.

'Whenever you get pregnant just make sure it's a boy. Say your prayers to Shivji Maharaj everyday,' Sarita's mother-in-law said over and over again, as she rested her aching back against the wall of their tiny two-room flat and asked her daughter-in-law to fetch her a fresh cup of tea.

Fortunately, Sarita learnt of a magical machine owned by a local doctor which could tell the sex of the child while still in the womb. And the clinic offered abortions as well. The relieved woman next door had just got it all done. She had saved her family from a third daughter and said it was quite simple.

Sarita decided to go to the clinic as soon as she had saved the 500 rupees that were required for the ultrasound scan. She would get the abortion done, if it was a girl – but pay the remaining 2,000-rupee fee over a period of one year if she signed a form, as her neighbour had told her. The doctor, it seemed, was very sympathetic towards poor women who could not make immediate payments. Only a very small interest would be charged if the payment was further delayed.

She waited for three months and scraped together the money. Fortunately she did not put on too much weight, so no one guessed her condition at home. Kishen was busy with some new feature film posters and her mother-in-law was too sick to get out of bed. Her father-in-law spent all his time smoking beedis and chatting with his friends and was not interested in her anyway.

To her horror, the magical machine said it was a girl. Sweating with fear, Sarita decided she had no choice and signed the form, saying she would return in a few days.

But her heart ached with longing for the unborn child. She sensed the baby growing inside her and mentally spoke to it all the time. She wondered how her mother had given her up when she was fully formed! How could she abort her unborn child? What kind of mother was she to think like this – she was worse than the dayen. She knew she couldn't ever kill her daughter after her birth, as some women did. Desperate ideas of running away with her child swept through her mind but she knew that she and her daughter would not be safe without the protection of a man. She was completely trapped.

Sarita's only hope was the dayen. She wondered if she could plead with her to keep the child in the orphanage just like Sarita herself had been kept. At least her baby would live! The idea appealed to her more and more. Perhaps she could go to the orphanage and deliver her baby there. And tell her husband and his parents that the child had been stillborn?

Plucking up courage, Sarita told her in-laws about the pregnancy and said that, since the orphanage warden had been like a mother to her, she wanted to go back to her to have the child in her familiar childhood surroundings. Because it was a girls' orphanage there was no question of Kishen or his family accompanying her.

As expected, the dayen was very happy to accept the grandchild of the devi who had died in the well. Perhaps the MLA would smile upon her once more. Lately he had lost interest in her problems and there were rumours she might be transferred to another branch of the orphanage. Her main worry was that the baby had turned out to be such a lovely child. She had to keep her well hidden or she would be stolen into adoption very soon. She forced only one promise from Sarita — as she had from Sarita's mother — that she would never come back to meet the baby, ever again.

Depressed and sorrowful, Sarita went back to her in-laws as soon as she could, as she did not want them to suspect anything. Kishen's parents, who were initially sad at the loss of the baby, recovered very swiftly when they learnt it had been a girl.

'*Chalo,*' sighed her mother-in-law philosophically, 'Whatever God wants. But at least He spared us the burden of a granddaughter.'

Only Kishen seemed to share Sarita's sorrow and actually cried when she told him of their daughter's death. He even made a large painting of a baby girl and hung it on a wall at their home. It was what he imagined the baby would look like — fair and chubby cheeked — with Sarita's blue eyes.

Sarita's own tears would not stop falling. But she was surprised and puzzled at her husband's grief and asked him why he wasn't relieved? After all, her mother-in-law had made it quite clear that she wanted a grandson.

Tears trickled down his cheeks as he said, 'I told you I had sister who died when I was still in school. She was older than me and she always used to look after me. Fed me before she ate, took me to school, even though she had to stay at home and help with the housework. Usually brothers look after sisters but for us it was the other way round – she protected me. My favourite day was raksha bandhan because she would make special sweets for me – ladoos, sweet paranthas. I loved her so much that I wanted a daughter just like her....'

'But your mother said...' Sarita whispered as her heart felt close to bursting. Her head spun, as the words died on her tongue. *What had she done?* 'Besides, don't you know,' Kishen added, not hearing her faint interruption, 'daughters are like Lakshmi... the moment they step into a home, they bring wealth with them. All our troubles would have been over if she had only lived.'

KISHWAR DESAI's debut novel, *Witness the Night* (Harper Collins India; Simon and Schuster) won the prestigious Costa First Novel Award (2010), was longlisted for the Man Asian Literary Prize, the DSC South Asian Literary Prize, the Waverton Good Read Award and shortlisted for the UK Author's Club Award, among many others. It has been translated into many languages and optioned for an international film. Her second novel *Origins of Love* was published in May 2012. Her critically acclaimed book, *Darlingji: The True Love Story of Nargis and Sunil Dutt* (2007), a biography of the iconic Indian film actors, covered 100 years of Indian cinema and history. She had previously worked in television as anchor/producer and her last job in TV was as Vice President, Zee Telefilms. She is presently completing her third novel, and a book on cinema on Devika Rani and Himansu Rai. She is also a columnist for *The Asian Age*, *The Week* and *The Tribune* and has published articles in *The Guardian* as well *The Daily Mail*, among others. But her only achievement of any real value is to be the lucky mother to Gaurav and Mallika Ahluwalia, both wonderful children.

Selected Poems

MEENA ALEXANDER

Mother, Windblown

Je cherche la chanson, je dois la retrouver…
Marie Etienne

I
Housekeeper

Why such wandering –
What has happened to home?

The ruinous everyday,
How to cope with that?

To have given birth once, twice,
And before that, to have borne witness

To a clot of blood
Drained into a china bowl.

It was up there in the mountains,
Where we loved each other,

Close to a forest of whistling deodar,
Deer too, ears pricked up.

II
Metal Mirror

To turn,
As if memory were a mirror (how trite it sounds).

But birds are pecking the air
Inside out,

A squall of pigeons and parrots
On loose stones,

Hammer toed quail, and horsemen
Desperate for conquest

Racing past women threshing millet
In the city of Iltutmish, in the year 1230.

Then and now
Markets crashed, painted birds flung back.

III
Interlingual

No, not that deaf, grave past,
Rather to be here where I have gone on

Saying yes, yes – always yes!
To reel backwards,

To be gathered (as the vagina bleeds)
Into unerring lightness.

Later, the mottled part,
The hair speckled part

Bejewelled and puffed up,
(Who made these colors?)

Translated
Into a mother tongue

Which no one can hear
For very long.

IV
Himalaya

Once a seven week creature
Paddling inside, scraped out.

Twice, a nine month creature
Thrust out, wailing.

Boy and girl, sticky and sweet
All sucking mouth and shit.

Later we were mother
And two children who had no boat

To cross the dark river,
Ferocious fastness

Wind pleated
At the foot of the mountain.

V
There is No Subject

It still hurts inside,
Light pulled up out of me

And a great light pressing down.
I don't now how else to put it,

Ribs thrust open,
The future impenitent.

Who will teach you patience
Scarlet sash

Culpable in beauty,
O extravagant umbilicus

Empress of all festivals.
In the mirror (needful now)

A doe shorn.
Quivering flesh,

Her work done.
Or not, not ever.

Coda (Sky-Water)

Borne north in dreams
There are lights in the sky, driven lights.

I swim freely
(Ponder the adverb)

Through a ring of gold
Encircling a boat,

Timbers splintered,
Winged boat

Found in a *Jardin des vestiges*,
What the Phoenicians fled

As death came calling.
On a cloudy slope

Deer nibble cut stalks
Of deodar and chir pine.

Syllables tumble
In a milky river:

Babbling mother
Font of memory.

c. Meena Alexander, 2011, Published in *Women's Studies Quarterly.*

Boy from Rum

A lad from Rum
Is lost in a garden of creatures
Who have no tongue.

They make music brushing wings,
Fleshly things that pour down the back,
All muscle and grit.

He stumbles through a mess of shrubs,
Comes upon a girl seated in a pavilion.
Her face is veiled in gold.

Under her flows a channel of milk.
My son comes with singing words
From the Duc d'Orléans who lived

In the same time as the boy from Rum
(Struck dumb in a garden painted
For a Muslim emperor, King of Kings).

My son who is tall and lean like
The lad from Rum, dressed though
In jeans and black wool jacket,

Plucks off his cap and sings
Quand je fus pris au pavillon,
Je me brulay a la chandelle, ainsi que fait le papillon.

He sips warm milk, nibbles at bruised
Cookies I have made for him.
Restless then, he plucks up the phone, and sings.

Does she hear,
An old woman, his mother's mother
Stooped at the edge of a veranda

Where monsoon mists pour?
Its night time there.
Someone sets a candle at her side.

No words only music,
This is my whole dream.
Dull witted moths spill into flame.

c. Meena Alexander, 2011, Published in *Weber: The Contemporary West*.

Everything Strikes Loose

In the end
everything strikes loose

Look at my hands
that held you
as the pepper vines
hold to the mango tree
my child, my first child.

What fuels the mind
I tell myself
is not grief,
not waste:
just a bird beak
scuffing up leaves
at the tree's base.

Yet see
the pepper vines slip,
roots clustering
colourless as air.

I plucked the first
fruits for you,
the sour stuff
you spat, the sweet
dribbled down your chin.

You were greedy then
'Amma!' you cried, pointing.

I could not see
if the blackness
at the pepper's core
had burnt you.

The glare
was in my eyes,
the flickering leaves,
the golden Pamba river.

Now the river trickles
through low hills,
it tastes of childhood

The boats fly no flags
the races are all done
and flat barges driven by men
bear cinnamon, cloves, dried pepper.

c. Meena Alexander, 1995/6 *River and Bridge*, (New Delhi: Rupa, 1995/ Toronto: TSAR Press, 1996)

South of the Nilgiris

My son who is young
just six this year
knows the red soil of our land.

Turning it in his palm
he said
'My sister is this earth
I am water
we will mix together.'

I heard this in a dream.

He pointed at my belly
watermelon swollen
streaked as if mud
had dribbled over
lighter flesh –

'I am glad
I was not born a girl.
I will never hold that weight
in my belly.'

He spun on his heels,
on his lean shoulders
I saw wings of bone
pale as the stones of Kozhencheri

'Mother!' he laughed
'You know I am not a girl!'

Under my ribs
she turned
his unborn sister,
green as a wave
on the southern coast
ready to overwhelm me,
overwhelm even the distant hills.

---

c. Meena Alexander, 1995/6 *River and Bridge*, (New Delhi: Rupa, 1995/
Toronto: TSAR Press, 1996)

Passion

I

After childbirth
the tenth month's passion:

a bloodiness
still shifting at her core
she crawls on the mud floor

past the empty rice sacks
blown large with dust,
rims distended like sails.

Her skin scrapes a tin bowl
with water from the stream,
a metal frame

bearing a god
whose black blue face
melts into darkness, as a gem might

tossed back
into its own
implacable element.

She waits,
she sets her sari to her teeth
and when the chattering begins

fierce, inhuman joy,
monkeys rattling the jamun tree,
bellies distended, washed with wind

she screams
and screams
a raw, ungoverned thing.

II

There are beetles scrabbling
in the open sacks,
chaff flies in the half light
a savage sound in her eyes
struck free

the human realms of do and don't
the seemingly precise, unalterable keys
dashed to a frenzy
and still the voice holds.

III

One summer's day
I saw a heron
small and grey
blinded by an eagle's claw

it dashed its head
against the Coromandel rock.

The bleeding head
hung on
by a sinew or two
as the maimed bird

struck
and struck again

then turned to rise
an instant
on its sunlit wings.

It was carved in bronze
against the crawling foam

agony
the dead cannot know
in their unaltered kingdoms.

IV

I am she
the woman after giving birth

life
to give life
torn and hovering

as bloodied fluids
baste the weakened flesh.

For her
there are no words,
no bronze, no summoning.

I am her sight
her hearing
and her tongue.

I am she
smeared with ash
from the black god's altar

I am
the sting of love
the blood hot flute
the face
carved in the window,
watching as the god set sail

across the waters
risen from the Cape,
Sri Krishna in a painted catamaran.

I am she
tongueless in rhapsody

the stars of glass
nailed to the Southern sky.

Ai ai

she cried.

They stuffed
her mouth with rags

and pulled her
from the wooden bed

and thrust her
to the broken floor.

I, I.

---

c. Meena Alexander, 1995/6 *River and Bridge*, (New Delhi: Rupa, 1995/ Toronto: TSAR Press, 1996)

MEENA ALEXANDER was born in Allahabad, India and turned five on the Indian Ocean. Her childhood was spent both in Kerala and Khartoum. At eighteen she went to England to study; afterwards she lived and worked in both Delhi and Hyderabad. For several years now she has lived in New York City. Her new book of poems, *Birthplace with Buried Stones* is forthcoming from TriQuarterly Books/Northwestern University Press. She is the mother of a son, Adam Kuruvilla, and a daughter, Svati Mariam. Motherhood has made and unmade her, stitched her together and torn her apart. She is haunted by what it means to live as a daughter, and as a mother. www.meenaalexander.com

Missed Call

NISHA SUSAN

Last night, two squabbling cats leaped on my son's chest. They bounced out of the corridor and landed in the dark on Vijay who was sleeping with his head in the room and the rest of his body in the corridor. He was scared shitless and by the morning he was burning with fever. I told him to stay at home from school, but I also couldn't help ragging him a bit. He's very tall now, nearly six feet, and working at a gym after school so that he can body-banao for free. He didn't fancy my teasing him at all.

It doesn't help that his younger brother is scared of no living creature and is constantly catching scorpions and strange insects and making kissy noises at the baby shark that's growing at an alarming speed inside our fish tank. The fish tank, too, has grown at an alarming pace in the house. At first, we had the little one that Ritu Madam had given us when she left Delhi and moved to a Pune school. Manu was six then. Some of the staff had looked peculiarly at her, no doubt thinking, 'Do you really need to give the cafeteria cook who lives in some slum a fish tank?' But Ritu Madam understood Manu even then. Today the fish tank is almost a third of the room. When we bought our TV we could only get a size and shape that would not eat into the space for future baby sharks or whatever other forsaken animal Manu would bring home.

Manu himself wouldn't have teased his elder brother about the cats. It's just Vijay's pride that's been hurt a bit. In these last six months he has grown into thinking of himself as a man. He's almost sixteen. He told me, in as many words, when I had my accident: 'Now, ma, you be our child for a while.' No one knows that in the first month he had to wipe me down, help me walk across the corridor to the loo and steady me as I squatted. He even washed my blood-stained underwear for a week. Funny now that I think of it. Radha, who went to work at the parlour, even the day after my accident, never thought to ask how I managed all day. She must have thought it was a good thing her brothers were home from school to help me and left it at that.

Everyone in Begumpur told me, 'You're so lucky that when the car hit you the driver stopped. Who takes responsibility these days? Who takes someone to hospital and pays for all the treatment?' I never disagreed, never let on that I didn't feel grateful for two broken collarbones and a cracked hip, though I did feel grateful for my good, smart children who took care of me. I kept smiling the same way I had smiled a few years ago when people told me that as a widow I shouldn't splurge on renting a second room. I kept smiling when they told me I should save money for my daughter instead. I wasn't going to tell them the extra room was to ensure that daughter and sons didn't tangle their legs under the bed. I laughed and looked foolish and let my neighbours walk around feeling smarter.

Sometimes you wish you didn't know things about your children. I knew my daughter would have loved to have the regular set of mother-father pushing her to get married from the time she was sixteen. Sadly for Radha, I told her early on that there was going to be no dowry and no huge wedding. But I'd somehow find money to pay for her to study whatever she wanted, I promised. Radha thought this was me being cunning. She knew that I knew that she didn't want to go to school at all. When she came home bristling her thin, flat chest and demanding I pay for a beauty parlour course, she must have thought I'd refuse. I agreed right away and only asked to go to the parlour and speak to the woman about what she'd teach Radha for six months. Radha looked a bit deflated then, but it was a good choice on her part. She goes to the parlour every morning with a bounce and a whistle that I've never seen in ten years of her schooling. She's nineteen and truly relishes having her own money to buy a cellphone. Or recently the home pedicure kit she's been unleashing on the neighbours. Perhaps her disappointment that I wasn't going to be like the parents of her jigri dost, Guddi from the next lane, would lessen with time.

Guddi's been married two years now. When she returns home from Faridabad once in six months, she comes in eye-watering orange and magenta regalia, determined that no one should forget she's a married woman now. As if I hadn't known her when she was a nine-year-old who gave my daughter headlice. As if I didn't know that this summer, when the water stopped coming in her parents' lane for 15 days at a stretch, her father told her: 'Stay at your sasural, don't visit us in the summer anymore.' His pride couldn't bear her borrowing two mugs of water from the neighbours to wipe herself every morning.

I had my own reasons for wanting Guddi to leave. I was lying in bed a few weeks after the accident – hot, achy, uncomfortable – when I overheard her and Radha gloating over Guddi's husband's victory. He'd finally bullied his father-in-law to buy him a new motorcycle. 'Now I can hold my head up again,' said Guddi. 'I was sick with shame when I realised Papa thought he can get away with a scooter the way he had with both my didis. Who rides a scooter these days?'

I heard my daughter giggling loudly in agreement. Who rides a scooter? Nobody, I thought. Certainly not Guddi's presswala father, who's been cycling three kilometres to his stand under the tree in Malviya Nagar for twenty-five years. I wanted to get out of bed and slap Radha and Guddi.

I've never hit my children and now was hardly the time. And besides, in the late evenings my body hurt the most and I was at my most irritable. I told myself I *had to* rest for my bones to knit together so that I could get back to work.

The school was not cutting my salary for my first month in bed. And then school closed. But when school reopens, they might hire someone else. Never mind how much they say they love my cooking and how they put my picture in the annual magazine three out of the fifteen years I've worked there.

In a while Manu came home, and then Vijay. I thought I heard a flirtatious note in Guddi's greeting to Vijay but that was just me being a crazy old bitch. She's always been fond of the boys since she has no brothers herself. They're not bad girls, Radha and Guddi.

This morning, my aches were not much better. The children were a little tired of their own limited cooking and were grumpy. I creaked out of bed, crouched over the single burner and made the pretty yellow dal with flecks of palak they secretly like almost as much as Maggi. Vijay insisted he was fine and dressed for school. Having managed to stay on my feet for a bit, I didn't want to go back to the sweaty bed. I walked about a little in the corridor.

Gulshan from the floor below was standing in his baniyan-chaddi drying his clothes on the railings of the metal stairs. I looked away, partly to avoid his gaze and partly to avoid looking at the staircase. In a few weeks I'd have to go to the hospital again. The thought of getting up and down these stairs made me want to weep. When the ambulance first brought me back to Begumpur, I had to be carried up like a sack of rice. The boys couldn't manage, poor skinny things. Gulshan's older brother and Gurpreet, the landlord's nephew and two other men I didn't recognise from the street groaned and huffed as they heaved me up the five flights. As I was turned around the third landing, I saw Manu biting his lip as he followed us. I caught his eye and in a flash of understanding, I knew he was trying not to laugh at his elder brother. Poor Vijay was mortified to be dependent on other men to help his mother, and even more so because he wasn't sure if the men were copping a feel of his mother's fat ass. Manu's rolling eye was making me laugh, my broken hip stabbed me like a sword and I cried instead. I had forgotten about that moment till just now.

Behind me I heard Radha say bye and clatter down the stairs almost before I could lever my whole body around to face her. I turned around again and went closer to the railing to see her walk down the street. There she went, already missed-calling on her cellphone, blithe as she pleased, a tiny, smug smile tugging her lips. The missed-call operation baffles me and enrages me almost equally. Radha, for instance, never actually calls me when I'm at school. She only gives me missed calls and expects me to call back. 'No balance' is her perpetual excuse. Radha, Guddi and gang all have missed-call codes for each other. So many rings for whatever message.

Then there are the boys who just ring random numbers and say hello-hello until they reach idiot girls like Guddi and Radha who coo back, 'No, *you* tell me your name first. No, why should I tell you who I am? Where did you get my number? No, my name is Guddi. There is no Sonali here. It's *Guddi*. I live in Begumpur. No, I'm quite fair. No, I'm not Sonali, I'm telling you. Hee hee. *You* shut up.' After a couple of times of listening to this radio drama I thought the top of my head would come off like a faulty pressure cooker. I screamed at both of them that only fools would start romancing wrong numbers.

The hospital visit was more disastrous than I'd expected. I hadn't realised how scared I'd be crossing the road. I kept feeling the car hit me over and over again. Back home, on the stairs up, I stumbled and fell and banged my knees. Vijay felt guilty for not preventing it, and so he'd been snapping at me. Manu skipped up to me and told me with unusual seriousness, 'Ma, you must lose weight. I saw on TV that if you become thin, you won't get heart attacks that easily.' Heart attack. I could hit that doctor for throwing that phrase about in front of the boys after checking my blood pressure. It is a bit high, my BP, but how can I cook without tasting for salt when I go back to work?

When Radha came in, I was feeling very sour. I've been telling myself recently that I must not become one of those women who've forgotten what it was like to be young and happy. But Radha's hints about marriage have been exploding and flying about the house like mustard seeds lately. First, there were the Three Days of Tragedy. From what I pieced together from eavesdropping and police-procedure interrogation, her current love interest is a friend of Guddi's husband. He's in the cellphone repair business in Nehru Place and has won the girls' hearts by regularly giving them movies they can watch on their phones. Now they no longer had to go to the guy who hung out on the Begumpur main road and pay him to transfer any new movies into their phones. All the neighbourhood parents suspected that he mostly stocked blue movies so it wasn't that easy for the girls to go to him undetected.

Radha and this new guy — their thing's been going for a few months and, of course, he truly loves her. So much so that the first chance he got, he agreed to marry some girl his parents had picked. For three days, Radha refused to go to work, crying, weeping, staring into space and, to my shock, she refused to even drink water. If I could've got out of bed I would have prised her jaws apart and stuffed food down her. Manu, always the clever one, made fun of her the fourth day saying, 'Didi, you're so thin you look like a boy anyway. Now I don't know what'll happen. Who'll marry you?' Radha threw a plastic bottle viciously at his head. Manu was hit quite hard but refused to hold a grudge. He laughed loudly and went to school. Radha ate something.

That evening, Manu came home from school with a furry, white rat in a box. Before I could exert my ritual sacrcasm about his zoo, he announced that his English teacher had asked his address so he could come and enquire after my health. Vijay growled, 'Of course, of the sixty kids in your class your teacher wants to come and visit only your mother when she's stuck in bed. Tell him that we may not have a father but our mother is not unprotected.' I wanted to laugh but I held it in. I looked at the floor and tried to look grave and grateful, but Manu saw me smiling. Radha looked at me speculatively.

In a moment of weakness that night when we were both ready to sleep, she told me that if only she had been the right caste, Manoj would have married her for sure. For once, I held my tongue in the dark and didn't tell her how stupid she was. And who knows, maybe she was right. Maybe to some young men caste does matter as much as love. Raja and the boys I remember from my teens in Jharkhand, God bless them, they never discriminated. Any girl who would put out and had the right body parts was good enough for them. Raja didn't even care I was Christian when he married me. 'I just want the right to squeeze your thighs when I feel like,' he'd whispered into my ear as we rattled about on the floor of the train to Bhopal.

Encouraged by what she thought was my forbearance, the next day after work, Radha told me that she had talked to Him again. He'd consoled her that they could still be together even after he got married. This time I was speechless with rage. Radha mistook this for some sort of Guddi-like complicity. She thought I was her friend! She babbled on about how she'd spoken to him for two hours on the phone and had snuck out of the parlour early feigning illness to meet him. Soon everything would be alright, Manoj had promised. I rolled over in bed and faced the wall. Radha didn't notice at first.

After a while she put her stick arms around me the way she used to as a child and tried to hug me. The girl was so pathetically skinny. What kind of mother was I that I couldn't feed my daughter and make her look like a woman? Perhaps I could cut parts of my excess flesh and give it to her. The insides of my head went dark with anger and I suddenly shoved her hard. Radha fell down. I looked down from the bed at her shocked little face. 'I don't want to hear anything more about this Manoj,' I told her. 'He sounds like a useless loafer. What does he mean by saying you can still be together when he's planning to marry someone else in a few months?'

She screamed at me then. What a terrible mother I was. How I'd sent her father away to die. How if she had a father she could have been married with a home of her own. How I preferred the boys to her. She had to work for a living so that the boys could go to school. I screamed back that she'd certainly never given a rupee to the boys from her earnings. She yelled that she'd always known I was jealous of her. I was a fat woman cooking for years and I only earned a little more than she earned at the parlour. On and on until the landlord's wife came up looking extremely upset. I hated having to see her when I was sweaty, unwashed and close to tears. Next year, when her middle son got married and brought home a bride, for sure she would use this fight as a reason to evict us.

I wronged her there. Gurmeet knocked Radha lightly upside the head and told her to go breathe some fresh air on the roof. And pluck some pudina leaves from the pot while you're there, she said. Radha went up heaving and sobbing. Gurmeet didn't say much, asked me if I was feeling better, muttered something about unmarried girls and left.

Radha didn't talk to me for a week. Not even when the neighbours came running saying there was a snake in the building and they wanted Manu to catch it. I pretended the fight hadn't happened and went on as usual. I didn't attempt to win her over either. She refused to sleep in the same room with me. She bullied Manu into sleeping on the floor next to me and went to sleep in his place before Vijay could object. Vijay was moderately respectful of his sister, but he was a greater stickler for propriety than even me. He didn't like her being rude to me. Then he got into a fight with her because she was on the phone half the night. He told me huffily that she'd been on the phone with 'Woh', demanding his fiance's number. Clearly, 'Woh' had thought this was a very bad idea and had refused. Back and forth the missed calls went. And the tears and the hissing fights and Radha's attempts to somehow finangle the number out of him. Vijay said, 'I don't understand what didi is up to. She

kept telling him that she wants the number *just like that.*
That she wouldn't call the other girl. That doesn't make any
sense at all.'

The upshot of this was that Manu and Vijay ganged up
and refused to share a room with her. She was back, stuck
under my nose. By then, though, I was just fed up with her
brainless behaviour. I wished I was better and could go to
work and get away from the children. On the other hand,
perhaps the accident had happened so that I could be at
home and see what my children are up to. I dismissed the
sentimentality instantly.

After a day or two, Radha unbent and began talking to
me again. We had a bit of a stumble one evening but that
too didn't last long. She came in beaming soon after and
said, 'Ma, look at my face.' I was trying to clean the room
without breaking my hip again. 'What is it?' I asked. 'Guess,
guess,' she said. 'Look closely. Don't you see any difference?'
I regret it now but I snapped, 'I don't care what you've done
to your face. I'm not interested in this beauty rubbish. I just
like to see healthy, happy faces.' Radha was instantly miffed
and who can blame her?

But the next morning she woke up in a great mood.
I was standing near the stairs as I watched her go. All the
way from the fifth floor, from the end of the lane I could
hear her brain humming like a hill of red ants. My stomach
clenched and unclenched at the thought that I'd begun to
dislike my daughter.

How ashamed my mother would be of me. She had such
pride in us girls. As much pride in me as she had in my
older sister, even though some birth defect kept didi like a

ten-year-old all her life. But my mother always praised her for helping in running the house: helping our grandmother in cooking, cleaning, fetching things, washing clothes.

My father had no doubt about how my mother would react when she heard the news when she came back. She had been away a week in Ranchi accompanying the staff of the school she worked in. And a week was long enough for one of my half-brothers to settle in like a fat snake in our house. Papa was fond of his sons from his first marriage, but mother's steady gaze usually kept them at a distance. In the middle of that week, when I came home after school I found my bastard half-brother squeezing and poking and twiddling didi. She, poor thing, was alternately laughing and crying and afterwards told me that he'd done this to her the previous day too. I was ten, so didi must have been sixteen then. I told my grandmother and my grandmother tore into the bastard and told him to leave the house. But he thought he had the measure of my grandma, so he stuck around smirking at us women. My father, on the other hand, had no doubt about what his wife would do when she returned. He didn't shout at his son or slap him as I thought he would. Instead, he pulled some money out of the pockets of a fraying pair of trousers hidden in the back of a cupboard, went to the backyard and found my half-brother. He thrust the money at him and told him to leave town immediately. 'Catch a train to Patna,' I heard him say clearly when I followed him to the backyard hoping to see my half-brother bleed from his nose.

That night, I told my grandma I would no longer make rotis for my father, and she only said, 'Alright.'

The next morning my father asked for a glass of water and I ignored him. The truth is, I've never spoken to him since. My mother, back from Ranchi after the school trip, heard the news from us. She was so terrifying in her rage that none of us dared speak to her. After a few months she calmed down and resumed her normal, clipped exchanges with Papa. Didi accused me in her piping voice several times of being mean to our father. Papa could not hide his winces whenever she'd say this. He tried over the years to bully me into forgiving him but I never did. I didn't go to his funeral even. My mother never asked me to.

The only time my mother was truly ashamed of me was when I first tried to run away with Raja. It gave my father, my uncle and one of my half-brothers permission to beat me up, permission to tie Raja in a sack, ready to drown him in the river. I had to sneak out of my house and get to the sack before they did. Raja and I left home again that night. Six months later we were in Delhi. Six years later, I had two children and a cleaning job in Ritu Madam's school lab. Seven years later, I had three children, a cleaning job in the school canteen and the satisfaction of kicking out a cheating husband. I didn't go to his funeral either, and I'd be hard-pressed to tell you what he died of.

Lying in bed with nothing to do was making me maudlin. I spent too much time thinking of the past.

I was at that odd stage of recovery when I was too unwell to do much but too healthy to be patient anymore. It's the kind of mood in winter I'd assuage by busting my budget on red carrots. The slow, patient making of gajar halwa made me feel better on the days it was too cold to do much else. But summer in Delhi with three broken bones and a cast? I wouldn't wish this itch on my worst enemy.

Vijay must have sensed my restlessness when he came home. Perhaps because they had no father, perhaps because we'd been living in each other's armpits in the kind of houses we could afford in Delhi, or perhaps because I had them so young my children have always been sensitive to my moods. Vijay asked me to help him draw diagrams in his science lab book. I taught all three kids to draw but lately I've needed to do very little of it. I taught them to read English too, by getting Ritu Madam to teach me first. After I finished one diagram I was exhausted. Squinting and holding the pencil carefully had wiped me out. I fell asleep without eating dinner. I woke up at some point and found all three kids crouched like baby owls in the dark, watching TV at the lowest volume possible. The fish were still in their shoals but the baby shark swam restlessly and gleamed at me.

All of the next day I was tired and restless. I cleaned both rooms slowly: dusting, folding, wiping, sweeping. I spent the whole day doing it. It was by accident that I found my savings certificates in Radha's trunk carefully folded between her two best chunnis. It was the Rs 20,000 savings certificate Ritu Madam had put in my name before she left for Pune. I dug around more and also found my passbook in there. I tasted a backwash of one of the pills I'd eaten that morning. I quickly looked at the last page and found no new entries. The Rs 50,000 I had saved pai-pai for the kids' education was still there.

I retrieved the papers and put them back in my trunk.

When Manu returned from school I asked him to help me move the TV; I hid the papers underneath it. He was puzzled but didn't ask why his mother was looking crazed.

When Radha came home, we had a doozy of a fight. She showed no guilt, no remorse. She had only questions. Why hadn't I told them I had all this money squirreled away? Why had I lied that there was no money for a dowry or a wedding? What was I planning to do with the money? Unfortunately, it became a three-way fight because Vijay walked in unusually early from the gym. He was nursing a sore thumb from a weight he'd dropped on it. I've rarely seen him so angry. 'You keep quiet, didi. Ma doesn't need to explain herself to you. She doesn't need to give her money to you so you can give it to that useless Manoj. That's what this is about, isn't it? I know. I called and spoke to Guddi didi's Ranjeet bhaiya and he told me Manoj's family has already spent the dowry on fixing up their house, so he'll *have* to marry that girl. And if you find some money and give it to him, then of course he'll happily marry you. Why would you marry him? He doesn't even have a proper job. That cellphone repair shop threw him out last month.'

Radha screamed and tried to claw Vijay. I jumped out of bed but only managed to knock Manu over and wind him. He scrambled up and stood protectively in front of the fish tank. I almost laughed. Vijay was holding Radha's hands together in one of his giant hands. 'Don't hurt your sister,' I said sharply. But Radha was beyond protecting. She spat and wriggled and raged, the sparkles on her salwar suit making me feel slightly dizzy. Vijay let go and she tried to go at him again. 'What do you know about love, you giant black monkey? Who could love you? God knows who your father is. God knows who she slept with and produced you.'

It would've been better if she'd just clawed Vijay's eyes out. The poor boy was so sensitive about being dark like me when his siblings were fair like their father. After years of telling him that everyone from our family was this colour, I'd even caved and let him buy his creams. Not that they worked. I wanted to wring Radha's neck. The girl seemed possessed by a demon. Then I registered what she'd said, that I'd cheated on her father. I looked at Vijay and saw from the downturn of his mouth that he would always wonder if it was true. And just like that, in the flutter of an eyelash, the demon was inside me.

'Radha,' I said with such coldness and calm that she stopped shoving Vijay and turned to glare at me. 'What I do with my money is my business. Perhaps I might've given some of it to you some day. But you've clearly lost your mind. So you have two options. You can go back to living under my roof with my rules – as you once did. Or you can leave now.'

Radha's eyes grew as big as plates, like the faces in the cartoons Manu still likes to watch. She tugged her hands free and stomped off to the other room. The boys slept scrunched up like prawns on the floor of my room. The light stayed on and none of us had the energy to switch it off. From the next room, we heard fragments of conversations. At first there was passion and force in Radha's voice. As the night progressed we heard only whines and moans. We didn't stir or speak.

Around dawn I woke up to the sound of Radha's voice. She was still on the phone? 'What is the point of saying that you wished I was your daughter, Shefali didi, if you won't help me? I need to leave this house. I can't breathe anymore. I can't eat. I can't sleep. I have to leave. No, I don't want to wait till morning when I come to the parlour. I have to leave now. No no, I'm not coming to the parlour. No. Bye.'

I felt like the car that hit me was now parked across my chest. Should I cry? Will crying show her that her mother loved her? I couldn't remember the last time I cried. If you didn't count weeping from pain after the accident.

I could hear her charging in the next room. Manu woke up at some point. He fed the fish, pulled the single burner out and made Maggi for all of us with the same dispassionate efficiency.

It never feels like these times will ever end, but fortunately they do. We were all tightly sprung like coils the first few days. Radha came and went without explanation. The boys skirted around her. More days passed. We had our first conversation. She began sleeping in my room with me again. I had another hospital visit. I could go back to work in a week, the doctor said. I prayed the drama would end before my long work days began.

School reopened and I only missed a few days of work before I rejoined. It felt good to be standing square before my stove again. I got them to put a chair in the kitchen so I could cut vegetables and knead atta sitting down. Class IV made me a huge get-well-soon card for craft class. Radha made fun of it, saying that only Manu's art was worse than theirs.

Was Manoj back in her life or not? I wasn't sure and I didn't want to ask. I saw her watching movies on her phone and guessed that perhaps he was. But the missed-call drama was playing less, so perhaps he wasn't. I even briefly wished Guddi was around so I could grill her. I made a note to myself to go visit Guddi's mother. Sanctimonious cow though she was, she at least knew what her daughter was up to.

After a week at work I'd almost forgotten about my accident. Vijay's crushed thumb, though, just wasn't healing. I had to kick him all the way to the doctor. He came back looking terrified. The doctor had told him that in a few days the thumb would've been so infected he'd have had to cut it off. I was a bit sceptical but I didn't contest it, given that the results were a nice, clean bandage and no more ooze. Radha took over the cooking grudgingly though she still ate painfully little.

The next day I came home and cleaned furiously. I must have overdone it because a few hours later I collapsed into bed, entirely unable to move. I slept soundly and dreamlessly. I woke up when Radha came in with her jangle and her bangles. She said something about rotis and I grunted and went back to sleep.

I woke with a start, I don't know how much later, and went into the other room. Radha was crouched over the single burner holding a phulka; it bloomed over the flame. I opened my mouth to ask about the rather rancid smell coming from the stove. She heard me enter and, startled, looked up with those big brown eyes that are so like mine. The fear on her face knotted my stomach and there was an ugly, metallic taste in my mouth. The demon in my head wanted to know, 'What's in the rotis? What is she doing?'

With a vicious anger I'd always known in me, I smiled at my frozen daughter. I swooped up the whole stack and flung it into the corridor dustbin. Radha straightened out of her crouch and trembled. And then she was gone. I heard her thin chappals clattering down the metal spiral. I went to the railing and saw her run down the street, her handbag and chunni leaping behind her.

I watched her and remembered my father handing my half-brother money for the train. When my boys came home I wasn't going to tell them I'd sent their sister to Patna.

NISHA SUSAN is a writer and critic based in New Delhi. She was Features Editor at *Tehelka* magazine and has also worked for several non-profit organisations. Her short fiction has been published by Penguin and Zubaan and she's currently working on a novel and a book on Malayali nurses. Follow her at twitter.com/chasingiamb.

A Grandmother at Large

BULBUL SHARMA

The joyous, teenage puppy love I feel for my five grandchildren far exceeds what I ever felt for my children.

There. I have said it after denying it to family and friends for a decade. As a mother you love your children. That is the universal truth. Who else would love these ungrateful, back-chatting, over-critical, forever demanding creatures except their poor mother?

But once you become a grandmother, the truth dawns on you suddenly like a pure ray of sunlight. In that golden moment, you see a chance to redeem yourself, to rethink your entire life.

It is like rewinding your life and erasing the mistakes with correcting fluid.

'I will a better grandmother than a mother. I will not make the same mistakes again,' you tell yourself. 'I will listen to what they say, however irritating, and answer the same question ten times without losing my temper. I will not tell them to become just like me or just like the person I wished I could have been. I will not nag them or force them to be a different person.'

I will restrain myself from saying. 'Why can't you play the violin like Sunita's daughter? Why can't you read those junior classics I bought you instead of playing games on the computer all day?'

This time round I will not nag, demand, order, mould or push. Maybe I did not do all those things as a mother but I certainly felt like doing them every minute of the day. Anxious and worried about my children, whether they were growing up to be healthy and wise individuals with good teeth and superior brains. They have, with very little help from their odd parents, turned out to be good human beings, intelligent and kind, BUT not as superior as my *grandchildren*.

I am amazed that my children have managed to produce such perfect children. I repeat: I do love them more than my own. I love them with a pure, selfless, unconditional love just the way a mother rat loves her ugly babies.

The truth struck me when, the other day, my daughter came to visit me with her two children, Naina, the ten-year old, and Shivam, who's five.

The children rushed in to greet me and I too, overjoyed, hugged and kissed them as my daughter stood quietly at the door. After ten minutes of happy screaming and shouting, jumping on my lap, them pulling my hair (a game we play) and me pinching their cheeks, I suddenly noticed her.

'Hey, I am here too, Ma,' she said a wry smile on her face.

I do love my children but not in the joyous, gleeful way I adore my grandchildren and every other grandmother I have spoken to felt the same.

'It was love at first sight for me,' said R, a journalist who often misses deadlines to babysit her twin granddaughters.

'No one told me it was like this' said M, eyes sparkling like a lovesick teenager. 'My whole life is Rehan. I do not care about anyone else.'

How often have you been caught and pushed into a corner by a doting grandmother, armed with a loaded camera of recent pictures of her grandkids? 'And this one is when he spat out his first mashed potato. Isn't he cute?' 'This one was taken when he peed on his grandfather's lap.'

What is it that makes grandchildren so totally lovable? Is it the fact that you do not have to bring them up? There are no day-to-day hassles, irritations and frustrations as they refuse to eat, throw their food up on your best sari, make you trip over their toys, or behave badly when guests arrive or, worse, in a public place where you cannot give them a ringing slap. Then the trauma of sleepless nights when they are ill and you are out of your mind trying to cope. Terrible thoughts race through your head. 'What if…? Oh God… is she breathing? Why is he coughing so much… could it be… pneumonia/whooping cough/ Grey's disease, diphtheria or something congenital inherited from their father's side?'

I often think grandmotherhood is motherhood minus the trauma. It is sheer bliss to play with your grandchildren, spoil them silly as their parents watch with sullen disapproval and then go home, leaving the poor parents to cope with the mess. There are, of course, a few rules grandparents should follow if they want the relationship to flourish.

Remember, if you upset the parents they may take away your visiting rights.

Never criticise the parents in front of their children however tempted you are to settle ancient scores.

Never forget the other set of grandparents: remember they are your allies when things get tough.

Never give the grandchildren chocolates/green-and-purple sweets/ice cream/potato chips before a meal.

Never contradict if a parent is trying to discipline the child, no matter how unfair you think it is.

Never say 'You also scribbled on the walls, you too spat your food out, you used to dribble too etc.'

But after having said that I have to confess that I often fail to remember these rules and behave just like my mother did when she came to see my children. She told them to forget about doing homework, allowed them to eat an entire bag of chips, followed by huge bars of chocolate while they watched a horrifyingly violent Hindi film, wiping sticky fingers on the sofa. My children threw up on the carpet and had terrible nightmares but how they loved their Dida for giving them these illegal, delicious treats. When I tried to stop my mother from breaking these house rules she attacked me. 'You were such a naughty child. How much trouble you gave me for no reason at all. These two are perfect angels!' she would say, much to the joy of my children.

To this day, my daughter claims that it was my mother who nursed her through chicken-pox, measles and various other childhood illnesses. She has forgotten those sleepless nights I spent pacing up and down trying to soothe a wailing baby.

I have had my disasters with the grandchildren too, I must confess, and my son, who has his great-grandfather's critical eye, calls me irresponsible and unreliable. It was after a badly managed babysitting episode where I allowed the children to sing till midnight. The truth was they would not listen to me and insisted on singing 'Ba Ba Black Sheep' on top of their sweet voices till late at night. One of them found a plate and a spoon to bang on and the trio rocked as I watched helpless with laughter. They only stopped when they heard their mother's footsteps outside the bedroom door. Then they fell asleep at once like babes in the wood. I thought it was very cute: the parents and the neighbours were not amused.

To reinforce my lack of authority and poor babysitting skills, I fed my three-year-old grandson something weird the other day. Left alone in charge, all I had to do was mix some powdery stuff with hot water and feed it to him. My daughter repeated the instructions several times before she left. 'Don't worry I can manage,' I said as she gave me a worried backward glance.

But it was not that easy. Never believe those ads where pretty young mums mix baby food to soothing background music and spoon them effortlessly to eager and clean babies. The minute I poured the hot water into the powder stuff it turned into a cement-like mess that resembled the strong grout I use for my mosaic projects. It stuck stubbornly to the spoon and would not let go till I scraped it off with my bare hands. This must have been the stuff the witch in Hansel and Gretel had built her house with: super-strong and durable. Anyway, the child meanwhile was howling with hunger, so I made the horrible goo into tiny balls and tried to feed it to him. At first he refused like all sensible men with good taste, but then when I said these were special 'ping pong' balls which would bounce about in his stomach all day, he immediately polished them off.

'What did you feed him?' asked my daughter.

'Oh, just that cereal powder stuff you told me to,' I replied nervously.

'But, Ma, he keeps asking me to give him pebbles and ping pong balls to eat. Sometimes I wonder if you ever gave us normal food to eat when we were babies,' said my daughter. 'Do you remember something called puppy dog's food you used to give us? What was it?' she asked. 'Was it dog biscuits or what?'

'No, it was bread, milk and jam… all mashed up. You loved it,' I replied coldly. 'Besides it was the only pudding I knew I how to make.'

Your children are never grateful, unlike grandchildren who return your love with pure, unbiased affection. They are never critical and judgmental like your children.

'Why must you laugh so loudly, everyone is looking at us?'

'Why can't you make cakes like Gautam's mother?'

'Your hair/clothes/cake look terrible.'

'You never let us have any fun.'

'Must you embarrass me in front of my friends?'

A grandchild will never say these things.

For grandchildren, their grandmother and grandfather are the best people in the world, at least till they are about eleven years old. They know from a very early age that these are the people who will spoil them rotten, give them secret gifts, including banned items, and are always a soft touch for anything. 'Mama says we can't have that' always works like magic to get whatever they want from the old softies.

When Naina, my eldest granddaughter, comes over to stay with me it is pure joy with no hidden agenda to improve her mind or anything. Though I try very hard to get her to birdwatch since my own children were not interested.

'A bird shat on my head once and all you did was ask me what colour its wings were. You almost killed us showing us an eagle's nest on top of the hill,' they complain quite unreasonably. Naina too watches birds with me but only because she does not want to hurt my feeling. 'Can we go now, Nani? We have seen it enough. It is the same bird and it is not doing anything at all,' she says after twenty minutes of watching a rare hornbill.

So we watch rubbish but funny programmes on television, discuss her friends, eat junk food and grumble about her parents' faults. The love I feel for her and the other four younger ones is totally without any anxiety or expectations. I am not worried whether I am a good grandmother or whether I am teaching her the right things because I KNOW I am doing the right thing. I am just myself and Naina, I think, likes that.

'You never scold me like Mama and Papa. You let me bathe in the rain, they would never let me. Nani, you are the best,' she says and my heart swells with joy. 'Though your tummy is as plump as a pillow and you have funny spots on your cheek,' she adds.

I am overwhelmed. There was never any praise like this from my children. Maybe an odd remark or two like:

'You are strange but I still like you,' said my daughter at age ten.

'You can draw better than all the other parents,' my son declared at age eight, after I worked all night to make his school charts.

After that it has been mostly down hill. I know they love me and will do anything I ask them to (within reason and at their convenience) but where is that jumping-with-joy elation when they see me?

'Go away, no,' wails four-year-old Samara when I try to leave.

'Nani, please come back soon. We miss you,' Naina emails me when I am away. 'Don't forget the presents,' her brother, ever practical, adds.

All my five grandchildren adore me. At least for now. Naina the eldest is like a friend who listens to my stories with rapt attention unlike my children who groan, 'Ma, not again, we have heard that one a hundred times.'

Shivam, five years, will sit with me and draw happily for hours. Samara loves me reading to her. She prefers my iPad to me sometimes but then returns to give me a hug. Prithvi and Shiv, my two-year-old twin grandsons, are my little heroes. The world cannot touch me, no one can hurt me, irritate or upset me when the twins are with me, one perched on my shoulder, the other on my lap. 'Dadi … so nice…' they say. I am not sure whether they mean the picture in the book we are looking at or the chocolate in their mouth. I believe with all my heart they mean – me (though the other day they saw a picture of Kareena Kapoor and said, 'So nice' with equal, if not more, enthusiasm. I was a bit hurt at the sudden betrayal).

A grandmother is the most special person in the world because she will love you with abandon, will overlook all your faults, feed you what you want and not what is good for you, listen to your woes without judging you, always take your side in a row with your parents, will give you money secretly and be there for you always.

My grandmother, a gentle and beautiful woman, was very deaf. She refused to wear her hearing aid and when I asked her why she replied.

'All my life I have heard your mother and her sisters talk rubbish. Now that God has made me deaf, I am thankful to him because now I do not have to listen to them anymore.' She cooked the most amazing vegetarian food for us and would pile my mother's plate with extra helping muttering, 'So thin you are ... so thin.' My beloved mother who was plump and pretty all her life, would blush as we sniggered.

While my grandmother never left home and died in the same house she had lived in for fifty years, I travel all the time, like most other women of my generation.

'Why must you travel so much?' is the only complaint I hear from Naina. 'All nanis should stay at home,' she says.

All dadis and nanis did at one time. They stayed at home, cooked, knitted, made pickles and minded the house. And when things got too much for them they took off for a long and difficult pilgrimage to Badrinath. But now, the new generation of grandmothers work, travel and play golf. They attend board meetings and fight cases in court. They topple governments, cover battle zones and swim with the sharks in the ocean. The new grandmothers may not be sitting in their rocking chairs, knitting endless booties, but they are still grandmothers at heart. They will drop everything to be with their grandchild. My friend, a senior journalist, travels half way across the world every summer to babysit her four granddaughters.

Wherever I am, my first thought when I wake up is 'I wish I could see Naina, Shivam, Samara, Prithvi and Shiv today.' Then I go back to sleep, happy in the knowledge that their parents are doing a great job looking after them so that I can enjoy them with all my heart when I see them. But do I want to look after them full time, deal with the puking, potty training, squabbling, wailing and teething troubles once more? No thanks: I have been there and done that. Now, I just want the good times, the fun times. While mama and papa are bread and butter, for all children, a grandmother is jam – soft, gooey and sweet. May our tribe always remain so – sometimes unreliable and irresponsible, often inefficient and clumsy but ever loving and devoted.

Bulbul Sharma is a painter and writer. Her works are in the collection of the National Gallery of Modern Art, Lalit Kala Akademi as well as in private collections in India, UK, USA, Japan and France. She has published many books including *My Sainted Aunts*, *The Perfect Woman*, *The Anger of Aubergines*, *Banana Flower Dreams*, *Devi*, *Eating Women*, *Telling Tales*, *Now that I am Fifty* and *The Tailor of Giripul*. Her books for children are *Fabled Book of Gods and Demons* and *The Children's Ramayana*. Her books have been translated into Italian, French, Chinese, Spanish and Finnish.

She conducts 'storypainting' workshops for special needs children and is a founder–member of Sannidhi – an NGO that works in village schools.

Bulbul became a mother when she was twenty-two years old and cannot imagine life without her children. She thinks it is the most vital, difficult, wrinkle-making, wonderful, heartbreaking and meaningful part of her being.

Childless, Naturally

Urvashi Butalia

It has been two years since the man I nearly married and I decided to part. On a balmy evening, the leaves stirring gently behind us, we sit in a restaurant talking. The heartbreak is over, the friendship intact. We talk about what we shared, why we decided to go our separate ways and then, he surprises me by saying: 'You know the one thing I do regret is that we would have had such lovely children, and you, you'd have made a fantastic mother, you're such a natural.' A natural? Me? What has he based this judgment on, I wonder, and what does it mean? It's true that I love children – I did then and I do now, indeed I only have to see one on the road walking with or being carried by a parent and I 'naturally' veer that way. But does that mean I had what it took to be a good mother? I'm not at all sure.

❋❋

Thirty years later. I am still single, I still love children. I've become familiar with the question: why have you never married? Don't you feel you need a relationship? Are you not lonely? Don't you want children? I'm not entirely sure I follow all the connections but the questions insert themselves into my head and I ask myself: do I want children? Am I missing something by not being a mother? Most friends I talked to actively wants this, she wants to feel life growing within her, she wants to 'give' birth, she wants to be pregnant, to hold the child within her, to be able to give love unconditionally, to have someone to look after her (and her partner) in the future, to experience the joy of motherhood. I feel none of these things. Does that mean I am a cold fish? That I have no feelings? Am I fooling myself when I say I feel no active desire to have children – am I saying this because, in truth, I want them, but I do not want to seem lacking in any way so I imagine I don't? It's difficult to say. I'm constantly suspicious of myself though and worry: am I really the contented person I think I am or am I just pretending?

❧

My friend's statement stays with me. It comes back to haunt me time and again. Am I such a natural? Then why is the desire for motherhood not growing inside me actively? I think back to my friends who talk about being able to love unconditionally. I think, well, this is not something I am unfamiliar with – why do people assume such feelings then only meant for children? My friends have children, talk of sleepless nights, of irresponsible husbands, unhelpful siblings, of school admissions, of careers given up, of grades and universities: I hear this all the time. And I hear the throwaway remark: 'Well, how would you know? You've never been a mother.'

❧

I've just got my first job. It's in a publishing house: my father goes to the general manager, a genial Bengali, and tells him that he had better look after his daughter. The general manager tells me this is the first time they have employed a woman in an executive position: normally they do not like to do this because women go off and get married and have children. He makes it sound like a crime. I promise him I will not do this. I keep my promise. Long after I leave my job. No marriage, no children.

※

My mother and I are talking. I worry for you, she tells me, what will you do when you grow old? Everyone needs someone. If you don't want to marry, why don't you just adopt a child? But is that a good reason for adopting a child I ask her, to have someone around when you grow old? And what's the guarantee anyway? No, no, she quickly switches tack. That's not why I think you should adopt. But just think what wonderful grandparents this potential child is missing out on! Good enough reason for adopting, don't you think? I take her seriously. Perhaps she knows more than I do, I tell myself, and I start to search out adoption possibilities. For a while, I am quite excited by the change in my life that this promises, but in the end, I do not have the courage, or the motivation. I give up.

※

I've set up my own publishing house, publishing books by and about women. I am fiercely passionate about this, it's what gives me joy, it's what involves me, I know this is what I want to do all my life. I want somehow to make a dent in the way the world sees women, to be part of that change. Is this madness, this obsession? Why didn't I feel this way about children? Or am I just deflecting an unfulfilled desire? I'm told motherhood is a woman's destiny, it's what completes her. So what's all this about publishing? But I don't feel incomplete, or that I have missed my destiny. Is there something wrong with me?

My friend Judith has been trying to have a child for many years. She's deeply depressed, the relationship with her husband is becoming more and more tense. She's gone through many miscarriages, they're both desperate for children, but they can't seem to have them. She and I talk one day, standing in the dark near a lamp post in a cold European town. Why don't you adopt, I ask her? How can I, she says, I'm not at all sure how I will feel towards the child if she is not mine. But she will be yours, I assure her. She may not be born of your body but she will be yours. We talk. I am passionate about the joys of adoption, the importance of it, the fact that 'naturalness' means nothing in motherhood. Once home in India, I write her a long letter, persuasive, eloquent. She tells me that went a long way in making her decide. Today she has two lovely daughters, sisters, adopted from the same country, and she's a bestselling author of a book on motherhood. Why was I so persuasive? I don't really know.

I'm with my friend Mona Ahmed, a hijra, at her home in Delhi's Mehendiyan, an area with two mosques, a madrassa, two graveyards, a dhobighat and many houses. A man till the age of eighteen, and then castrated and now a woman after a sex-change operation, Mona tells me that she has always, always wanted to be a mother. I wanted to hold a child in my arms, to feel life against me, to learn motherhood, to bring the child up, she says. In her early seventies now, Mona fulfilled the desire to adopt a little over twenty years ago when a neighbour died in childbirth and her husband had no use for the daughter she had given birth to. Mona 'created' a family, herself as abbu, father, her hijra friend Neelam as ammi, mother, her guru Chaman as dadi, grandmother. The assigned roles though were a bit more mixed up. It was Mona who was the real mother; she was the one who nurtured Ayesha, gave her a name, a birth date, an identity. I chose the 26th of January as her birth date, she said, for I wanted that she be free like India. And I learnt how to be a mother, she adds, I went every day to the doctor, the pediatrician, and asked her to teach me how to feed the child, how to burp her, how to bathe, change, what to watch out for, how to develop antennae about when to wake up, and so on. Can motherhood then be learnt? Is this what there is to it? What about the 'naturalness' of it to women? What about someone like Mona – abbu, father, but actually mother.

❊❊

Mona's daughter, Ayesha, comes to visit me. We talk about her life, a young girl, brought up in a hijra household, the father (Mona) actually her mother, the grandmother (Chaman) referred to as 'he' by everyone but Dadi, grandmother, to Ayesha. Can you imagine what it was like? she asks me. They gave me so much love, but a young girl growing up, she needs some things, she has questions to ask about her self, her body, who was I to ask? There was no other female, only these men/women, these people of indeterminate sexuality. I was so alone. Perhaps motherhood can't be learnt after all.

✳

On a Thursday morning Bina, the daughter of the presswallah across the road runs away. No one suspects anything till it's afternoon. She'd gone to school to sit for an examination, perhaps she's gone out with friends afterwards. But Bina is a 'good' girl, she does not go off without informing her parents, so as afternoon turns to evening they start to worry. Back at home in their community, they wonder whether to go to the police. They are afraid of scandal — suppose it is something innocent, the girl's just gone off somewhere and fallen asleep, why make her disappearance public? But in the evening, they learn that a young boy, the son of a neighbour, is also missing. Suspicion begins to solidify into certainty. In the end, a report is filed. Two, three days later, both are discovered in a neighbouring town, and brought back home. They swear that they wandered away innocently — went for a walk to the zoo, then a film, then, frightened that the parents would be angry, they boarded a bus and went off to a relative's house. Did you sleep with each other, the anxious parents ask in euphemisms, there is

no straight way to ask youngsters if they have had sex, no
real vocabulary. No, no is the vehement denial. The parents
are relieved: they don't stop to ask how the youngsters so
quickly understand what it is they are asking.

A month later Bina is pregnant. Her mother and I take
her to a nearby clinic, We try to tell the doctor that it was
an accident, but Bina is quicker than us. No, she says, it
wasn't my first time with this man. We're silent. Clearly she
lied to her mother and to me. Her mother is devastated:
I did so much for her, and this is how she pays me back?
I understand her grief, but I wonder too — all that stuff
about unconditional love, where did this notion of payback
enter the picture? How do children pay back? Bina has her
abortion, and remains persona non grata. The young man
disappears from her life, and soon after marries someone
else. Men's peccadillos are easily tolerated.

Two years later, she runs away again. This time with a
married man. His wife is unable to give him children, so
he marries Bina, brings her into the household. She gives
him two children, he is delirious. She's now married, and
a mother. Her parents are relieved and happy. Everything
is settled. She's a mother. No one will say anything now —
besides her husband also has money. Legitimacy and
wealth — a powerful combination. Later, she will finance
her young brother to buy a car and begin a taxi service.

❊❊

My friend from overseas is visiting. We're talking over
dinner. It's her son's birthday, she does not know whether
to call him or not, their relationship is difficult, tense.

She's no longer with his father, he resents her because he feels she does not give him enough time or attention, she worries that he has not yet found a job. She calls him. Happy birthday son, she says. They talk, with affection, and then, suddenly, without warning, there is anger, resentment, almost a kind of hatred. I knew it, he says, you always do this, you always want to make me feel small. She tries to explain, he will not listen, she's devastated, but struggles to keep the conversation open. It ends badly. Am I a bad mother, she asks me? Is it wrong of me to want a career? I have done what I could for him, I love him, but surely it is time he took his life in his hands? What do you think I should do? I have no answer.

❈

I'm at home. My mother, ninety years old, is unwell. She's becoming weaker by the day, she's unable to eat, she has to be helped to the bathroom. One day, as I take her to the bathroom and help to clean her up, she asks me, how will I ever repay you for this? And I ask myself, and her, why should she even think this way? She's spent the better part of her life being a mother not to one but four children, surely we owe her something? That old payback thing again. As she gets weaker, I find myself structuring my life around her needs: leaving the office to come home for lunch so she is not alone, putting her to bed in the evenings, staying with her, her hand in mine, till she is peacefully asleep, bathing her, cleaning her, feeding her, taking her for a walk, spending time with her... in other words, being a mother to her. One of my friends comments on this, *you've* become the mother. My women friends and I discuss this, we find that all of us are in similar situations, mothers to our mothers, becoming our mothers. Was this what was meant by it being natural?

\#\#

We're trying to fix a meeting for an NGO that I am on the board of. There are six of us who need to meet and we're juggling dates. One of us, a man, says a weekend is better for him as his young son is getting married and he will not be free earlier. The other one announces that she is about to become a grandmother, and suddenly people start trading stories about being mothers and grandmothers, offering each other stories of how wonderful it all is. I pitch in saying I don't know about any of this, and am told, don't worry, we'll make you an honorary grandma, no worries if you don't have children. How true, I think, I have no worries of that kind. I will never have to worry about which school to send my child to, or be forced to think of her percentages when it comes to entering college. Or deal with the deeper anxieties that all mothers must have to deal with.

\#\#

But relief isn't all. There's also concern. I've just seen a friend totally devastated at losing her young son. Barely twenty, he died in a freak accident, she is inconsolable, she feels a part of her has been torn away, wrenched out of her body almost. This too is part of motherhood, this deep, intense attachment, this terrible, devastating despair when you lose a child. Could I have coped with this had it happened to me? Useless to speculate, but a sort of fear settles around my heart for all the mothers who lose children – surely, I think, there can be no loss worse than this. There's relief too, perhaps a selfish sort of relief, at being childless.

✦

But there's also concern, a question. For years I have identified myself as a single woman. It's important to me this definition: singleness is, for me, a positive state, one that is not defined by a lack, by something missing, by a negative – as for example the word 'unmarried' is. But with this children business, we don't even have the language to define a positive state. I mean, there is childlessness and there is childlessness. How often have we heard that a couple is childless, that a woman who cannot bear a child is defined as barren. Why should this be? I did not make a choice not to have children, but that's how my life panned out. I don't feel a sense of loss at this, my life has been fulfilling in so many other ways. Why should I have to define it in terms of a lack? Am I a barren woman? I can't square this with what I know of myself.

✦

I recall one of authors we've published, a domestic worker called Baby Halder. She had her first child when she was barely thirteen. A child herself, she became a mother before she had time to even think. At some point, Baby, reflecting on her childhood, commented on how ephemeral, how brief it was. One afternoon, exhausted from playing host to her sister's suitors, Baby slumped against the wall of her home and reflected on her life. So brief was her childhood that she saw the entire history pass before her in a few moments. I licked every moment, she said, as her cow licks her calf, treasuring it. For so many of our young girls, despite laws that forbid it, motherhood comes even before they have stopped being children. Is this right? Why is this thing so valorized?

❦

Nothing is simple though. The newspapers have been full of the story of a Bengali couple in Norway – the Norwegian authorities have taken their two children away from them. If reports are to be believed, one of the children has something called 'attachment disorder' – he starts banging his head against the wall when he sees his mother. The papers speak of a tense, conflicted, sometimes violent relationship between the mother and the child. Finally, the mother is deemed unfit to look after the children, and they are handed over to their uncle. Back at home in India, the whole thing acquires other dimensions altogether – politics and nationalism enter the picture. The issue seems to be how Norway can decide on what is right and what is not for our children. In Bengal, the Child Rights Committee decides to give custody back to the mother. None of the reports in the papers says anything about whether the mother is competent to look after the children or not, or indeed how the children are being affected by this constant backing and forthing.

Whatever the rights and wrongs of this case, what concerns me is a different thing. On a membership-based

email network called feministsindia, there is a general sense
of relief that custody has been awarded to the mother. There
seems to be an assumption that the mother is the 'natural'
(back to that natural stuff again) guardian, the best person
to look after the children. It's not the rights and wrongs
of this particular case that worry me – my knowledge
of them is, after all, only based on newspaper reports.
What concerns me is this: as feminists, we've questioned
everything about the 'naturalness' of motherhood but here
we are, in a way almost unquestioningly accepting that
naturalness, not even entertaining the notion that mothers
can be violent, that they can be incapable of looking after
their children, or even unwilling to do so. I wonder what
is going on here – was the response of the Norwegian
authorities a culturally insensitive one? Or was it that they
believed, as often happens, only the father's version? Were
all media reports of the mother's supposed violence towards
her children then totally wrong? Or are we, as feminists,
reaffirming the motherhood myth? Where does the truth
lie? Is the relationship between a mother and a child always
a wonderful one? I have no answer to these questions.

❈

So what do we have in the end? The 'naturalness' of
motherhood? The 'curse' of childlessness? The dread
of barrenness? A life filled with lack, with loss of what
might have been? Or just another way of living? A choice,
happenstance, circumstance, call it what you like, but for
me, it's a happy, contented, fulfilled life, despite – or perhaps
because of – being what is called 'childless'. For those of

you who've doubted yourself about this, let me assure you, it's a good place to be.

URVASHI BUTALIA co-founded India's first feminist publishing house, Kali for Women, in 1984. She continues to publish and promote books for, on and about women in South Asia as the publisher of Zubaan. She has edited several collections, and is the author of *The Other Side of Silence: Voices from the Partition of India*.

The State Can't Snatch Away Our Children

HUMRA QURAISHI

It's been quite a journey; several setbacks, more than enough daily doses of emotional turmoil, rude shocks and their aftermath. Little laughter. Only absolute fools can laugh in such times…

Sitting back, reflecting on what's kept me going, it is my two children, Sarah and Mustafa, who I keep coming back to. I owe my actual survival to them. Cocooned in that emotional cushion they provided, I survived a rather painful marriage until I plucked up the courage to walk out and finally end it after twenty-eight long years.

Perhaps the only two constants in my life have been my children and my writing. Here again, I couldn't have coped with deadlines if my children hadn't been supportive, understanding. In fact, my daughter even learnt to type in a typing school tucked away in some corner of the market. So, many a time while I wrote longhand and was too tired to type it out, she sat at the good old Remington for me. While my children did their homework, I wrote my pieces. And my children managed to fend for themselves for days on end when journalistic travels took me to reporting assignments in the Kashmir Valley and other far-flung places.

It wouldn't be wrong to say that I grew up with my children. Sharing, unleashing, confiding, arguing, discussing everything on life and living – yes, I told them just about everything: high menstrual flows or dipping financial lows. Hopelessly romantic on those couple of occasions when I did fall in love, it was once again my children who heard the details I offloaded…

My bonding with them does have a definite set of backgrounders. For one, I was terribly lonely in a hopelessly mismatched marriage and needed someone to talk to. Also, my own relationship with my mother was similar to that typically prevalent in the majority of Indian families where only 'safe' topics were allowed, and nothing very personal could be discussed or spoken about beyond food and clothes or such routine things.

I come from an upper-middle-class family of erstwhile Avadh, what is now Akhilesh Yadav's Uttar Pradesh. Though my parents sent us – my siblings and I – to a convent (Loreto Convent in Lucknow), they tried maintaining all those traditional aspects of Muslim life. Rather nostalgically, I recall a *maulvi* sahib coming to our home every day to teach us Urdu and help us read the Quran. Eid was celebrated with much enthusiasm. My father worked for the government so, until he retired, we lived in government colonies – be it at Jhansi or at Lucknow – alongside his colleagues' families.

My father was an introvert, my mother the exact opposite. Our home was overcrowded with close relatives and even those only distantly connected. Life here revolved around food. The family *khaansama,* Zahid mia, began each and every day with this one-liner, '*Begum sahib, aaj kya pakkega?*' My father always made it a point for us to sit together at the dining table. In fact, he'd wait for long stretches till we showed up at that laden table.

Besides food, the other issue about which my mother was most particular, was discipline. Though father wasn't strict (in fact, he was gentle and extremely emotional), my mother maintained, or at least tried her best to maintain, a set of dos and donts. Those donts included a strict code vis-a-vis clothes and that perennial dictat: 'No meeting boys'.

I rebelled early: I didn't have much choice. In class ten, I fell madly in love, and although decades have passed, I still remember that lovelorn me... with my intense love affair lying sabotaged, trampled upon. For days, I'd sat in absolute shock, followed by a longish spell of sorrow, depression and pain. And then I rebelled, so very completely. There were constant showdowns at home, intensified by my characteristic outspokenness and defiance. I couldn't understand why I was not allowed to wear a sleeveless shirt or tight-fitting trousers and short blouses, or go cycling down the lane towards the park or those eating joints which, for me, doubled as crucial meeting places! No, there were no discussions or chances to explain my point of view... just those definite 'no's'. With that, the communication lessened and I was left feeling hurt and upset. Looking back, I can understand my hapless mother's apprehensions and concern for me but still I wish she had not come up with those near halts of all my possible adventures and even misadventures, and had at least tried to explain or reason things out.

Given this background and my basic temperament – I'm a stubborn Taurus, terribly romantic, a firm believer in spontaneity and have a rather black-and-white approach to life – you can imagine why I tried bringing up my own two children, Sarah and Mustafa, more like close friends. Not that I sat and read parenting books or discussed how children ought to be brought up with experts. But I do believe that anything and everything must be done with intense feeling and selflessness. Of course, I've had some very heated discussions with the two of them but isn't that a vital aspect of being emotionally close?

My children know details of those various attractions and distractions I've been through – and why not! After all, I'm made of flesh and bones and blood, together with a big heap of emotions. They are well aware of the twists and turns of my personal life because I'd made it a point to tell them. A mother should never give the impression to her kids that she is some sort of a demi-goddess. Whenever there was an emotional blow, I would simply tell my children. Many a time the three of us sat and sulked together.

It's because of this bond with my children that I have survived at all – survived not just some trying times but also two nervous breakdowns. The first took place over two decades back. My children were young but they did understand the pain I was going through and the fact they clasped my hands in their own little ones has meant so much for me. It was they who helped me recover.

I also believe in the 'let go' philosophy. As Khalil Gibran says,

> Your children are not your children.
> They are the sons and daughters of Life's longing for itself.
> They come through you but not from you.
> And though they are with you, yet they belong not to you.
> You may give them your love but not your thoughts,
> For they have their own thoughts.

Another aspect which looms large from my childhood was the impact of news trickling in of Muslims getting hounded during rioting. In my parents' home, as in most Indian homes, dark realities were seldom discussed. Not openly. Definitely not in front of children. But realities can never be brushed under dusty carpets and children do sense and grasp things. In fact, even now as I write, I can remember how some of those details came trickling in, right into my ears – it was one of those late evenings when my younger two sisters and I were lying sprawled under mosquito nets on our beds. My grandfather, probably certain we were asleep, sat discussing with my grandmother the horrific rioting ongoing in one of the locales of Uttar Pradesh, with Muslims getting killed and hounded by the PAC jawans. I must have been very young then and the impact was difficult to cope with. To this day, those stories of police brutality have stayed with me, getting compounded in recent years as I saw for myself these things taking place, frighteningly and frequently backed by that powerful nexus between politicians and the police.

Another reality lay right in front of us every summer,

when we'd travel down to Shahjahanpur to spend our vacations with my maternal grandparents. It was here that I first saw acute poverty and helplessness among Muslims. Around my *nana's* ancestral home an entire *mohalla* lay spread out, housing poverty-stricken Muslims... their children looked hopelessly thin and tuberculosis stricken, their mothers frail. Many of them would come to our home recounting stories of not just their dire poverty but so many insecurities of the worst kind. The Right-wing political mafia often called this township 'mini Pakistan', simply because it largely comprised Muslims. In fact, it was to Afghanistan that several of these families traced their roots as, centuries back, Afghan clans had travelled down to settle here. Now, of course, many more are reduced to second-class positions, even my own relatives who sit in the grip of despair. Perhaps it started with Partition, when many a Muslim family of Avadh fractured overnight and it was compounded by the ongoing tactics of communally charged politics. The partitioning of our country by the British changed the very course of these families, as one of them puts it, '... from rulers reduced to living in these hopeless conditions... no, not just the poverty but those glances thrown at you, at your children by these *police wallahs...*'

Yes, as a child, this reality hit hard. As I grew older, it got harder to cope as I saw and sensed very early in life that I belonged to a minority community which faced some very obvious communal biases. There was blatant discrimination on several fronts – at crucial levels, the police and local administration, invariably run by the hand-in-glove partner, the politician. And the tragic aspect is that these realities have definitely worsened in recent years. I didn't have to be an investigative reporter to find this out. I didn't even have to go into Muslim mohallas or gullies or bastis. I saw and heard and experienced it all right here, in our capital city. Yes, in the supposed prime government locales of New Delhi. In fact, soon after the demolition of the Babri Masjid, it was traumatic to remove the nameplate from outside our home which, at that time was situated on New Delhi's high profile Shahjahan Road, supposedly a high-security VVIP area. Why did we have to remove it? Because it carried a Muslim name. And there were more than rumours of communally charged right-wing mobs attacking Muslim homes. After all, during the anti-Sikh riots of 1984, the home of at least one senior Sikh bureaucrat was targeted in Lutyens' Delhi. And, after the Babri Masjid demolition, I'd done an in-depth feature for the *Illustrated Weekly of India* on how Muslim children studying in the best possible public schools of this capital city had to hear snide comments not just from some of their classmates but many a time even from some of their teachers. The Babri Masjid demolition had several Muslim mothers slash their children's names/ surnames just to ensure basic daily survival. Sadly this seems an ongoing pattern in several communally charged locales of this country where minorities sit insecure in that second-class position. The first to be rounded up whenever there is trouble are boys from Muslim bastis. As several mothers from Ahmedabad, Malegaon and Hyderabad have told me, 'The investigating agencies/police do not want to look "right"… even if there's a cracker burst our children are picked up... sometimes released after weeks or months but their names lie fitted in those police records, so they are picked up again for any crime reported in any area...' It's more than a known fact that young Kashmiris who step out of the Valley to study or work in different cities of this country are immediately looked upon with suspicion by the local cops and given a hard time.

Even in this day and age, weird stereotypes prevail about Muslims in India. That they produce like rabbits or swallow meat at every single occasion or don't bathe... So very often have I heard this half-query, half exclamation thrown at my face, 'You really a Muslim? You don't look like one!' What am I supposed to look like? Perhaps, doing farshi salaams or stuffing meat-balls into my mouth, if not gulping down biryani... or clutching at the arm of a bearded, achkan-clad, topied man with a brood of squabbling children. Communal poisoning is giving a fillip to this propaganda. Sadly none of those Government Commissions or even that specially set up Ministry for Minority Affairs are doing a thing to halt these stupid and bogus notions from circulating. An average Indian Muslim's lifestyle isn't very different from that of his fellow Indians – the only difference is that the Muslim feels a deep sense of insecurity. Mind you, this does not come from you or me or other apolitical Indians but from those who are at the very helm: communally inclined politicians and their partners – civil servants and the police who are at their command.

In fact, in the last few years I have attended several public meetings held in New Delhi about this. Organised by well-respected activists of this country, the focus is on this grim reality – the growing despair amongst Muslim and their constant dread of being profiled as terrorists, followed by denial of bail, torture, a biased investigation and trial, and extra-judicial killings. More wearing, even, are the daily doses of discrimination in education, employment, housing and public services... the list is long and ongoing. And in the last two decades, my journalistic journeys to the Kashmir valley, brought home another of those dark realities – teenaged boys/young men picked up for interrogation by the various security agencies. Not returning. Declared missing. Thrown into 'missing' slots, even though in all probability the reality is that their young bodies could not take the strain of interrogation tactics. Missing young men of the Valley is a serious issue and needs immediate attention. It has left families ruined, and mothers sitting in deep sorrow, shattered and yet waiting endlessly.

When I first met Parveena Ahangar, the Srinagar woman who is heading APDP (Association of Parents of Disappeared Persons), she told me about her young 'missing' son, Javed. Listening to her, I felt emotionally drained, wondering at the extent of the brutality today's governance is steeped in, where they do not even stop at snatching away our young. For this middle-aged Kashmiri mother, the battle has been ongoing since 1990 which is when her schoolboy son was picked by the security agencies from their home in Srinagar's Batmaloo locality and taken for interrogation. Javed never returned and there has been no official news of his whereabouts. Nevertheless, his mother awaits his return. Every single moment is lived with hope. Today Ahangar heads the APDP, the longest ongoing non-violent movement of parents whose children have been taken away by security agencies and have never come home. Hundreds of families sit ruined, coping with the trauma, but Ahangar is one of those women who will not give up the battle. As she says, 'All these years we have been living in sorrow… I keep unwell, so ill that I cannot close my eyes the entire night…we have exhausted all our resources in trying to locate Javed in the various jails of this country, appealed to every possible government authority, to politicians across party lines but there have been only disappointments… I'm not giving up and will fight till I'm alive…hundreds of parents are joining our organisation, looking for their sons who have been picked up by security agencies.'

But not many mothers are equipped with this level of grit and determination. Many, in fact most, sit crumbling but, naively, these hapless women refuse to believe their sons could be dead, killed by the ruthlessness that this system is capable of unleashing. Their words echo in my ears: 'To bury your dead son is one thing but to go travelling from jail to jail and those countless police stations, looking, is another of those sorrows…the State can't snatch away our children to throw them in missing slots!'

In fact, each time I interacted with a Kashmiri mother awaiting the return of her missing son, I returned heavy with a sense of deep anguish. The word they'd kept chanting was '*sabr*' (patience with much hope). This, coupled with surrender to the will of God, is what keeps them going.

Delhi-based academic Uma Chakravarti and the Jammu-based journalist and activist Anuradha Bhasin Jamwal have also travelled extensively to Kashmir Valley to connect with those APDP mothers who are waiting with '*sabr*' for their missing sons. In an interview with me (*Times of India*, September 11, 2009), Uma Chakravarti said, 'We need a judicial commission to probe J&K disappearances.' When asked why she had taken up the cause of the APDP, she said, 'I'd met Parveena Ahangar of the APDP and was deeply moved by her search for justice. Parveena embodied the tragedies of so many others like her: mothers, sisters, fathers, brothers and sons. I have never been able to forget her persistence in trying to get at the truth of her son's disappearance and her determination to hold the State accountable for its actions. She turned her own suffering into a cause with all the others like her, keeping track of all reported cases of disappearances and travelling to meet the families of the disappeared...' Elaborating, she went to the very crux: 'No one wants to address the Armed Forces Special Powers Act and the immunity it gives to the security forces, and that rapes, custodial killings and forced disappearances that will continue unless there is legal redress for violations of people's rights. The easiest thing seems to be to not react or to pick up an item for a little while and then drop it. The government keeps talking about dialogue and confidence-building measures but has done little in terms of action. The first thing it should do is to set up an independent judicial commission into disappearances so that the average Kashmiri and the individual families that have been pursuing the cases of the disappeared can have a sense of closure. This has been done in Sri Lanka to investigate the large number of disappearances in the 1980s. It will be the first step in pursuing State accountability. It will have a tremendous impact in Kashmir. It will demonstrate the government's commitment to a rule of law.'

Meenakshi Ganguly, the South Asia Director at Human Rights Watch and author of 'Everyone Lives in Fear', a report on the human rights situation in Jammu and Kashmir, said this to me in an interview about the missing young men of the Kashmir Valley: 'The family members of those that "disappeared" have been campaigning for years. Parents have died waiting for a lost son to come home. Wives live with the label of "a half-widow". These disappearances are a lasting wound in Kashmir, and we hope that families will finally have some answers and receive justice. Disappearances are among the most heinous of human rights violations because families are left without answers, caught between hope and despair. I have met numerous families that are still waiting for news of their loved one. Some keep hoping for a magical reunion. Others say that they want at least to be able to weep at the grave of their lost one....'

For me, personally, the biggest hope came two decades ago – in fact, the day after the Babri Masjid lay demolished. My school-going children had stayed at home, only to be joined by their friend, Radhika Subberwal, whose mother made it a point to drop her at our place to be with us on that crucial and tense day. From the safe confines of their apartment at the Ashoka Hotel (where Radhika's father was then General Manager) to our flat on Shahjahan Road... this, when she was well aware of the grim fact that it was a Muslim home and so could have been attacked in the aftermath of the demolition and rioting.

Yet, by making it a point to leave her teenaged daughter

in our home, that mother relayed an immense solidarity. I can't quite describe what great hope her gesture held out. It is because of people like the Subberwals that the fabric of our country is still intact. Yes, there is hope that human beings will not be further divided and will see through divisive political games and the havoc they unleash.

HUMRA QURAISHI is Amma to Sarah and Mustafa, and Nani to Ali and Hassan; she is a Delhi-based writer-columnist-journalist. Upheavals on the personal front provided a catalyst for her writing. She believes that, perhaps more essential than the daily dose of food or water or chai, it is emotional love and bonding that will carry you through turbulent times. Humra Quraishi's books include a short story collection, *Bad Time Tales*; a book about the Kashmir Valley, *Kashmir: The Untold Story*; and a volume of her collected writings, *Views, Yours and Mine*. She has also co-authored a book with Khushwant Singh entitled *Absolute Khushwant*.

Blankets in the Sky

ANDROMEDA NEBULA

'Don't dead people feel cold sitting on the stars, Amma?' asks my eight-year-old worriedly. Pat comes the answer from her know-it-all younger sister: 'They have blankets, stupid!' Reassured, she snuggles up to me and we continue to gaze at the constellations, over-the-top in their luminosity in the inky sky. The accursed load-shedding has its blessings too. We are often to be found out on the roof, braving the bitter cold, bathing in moonlight until the dew drives us indoors. Star-gazing, lessons on gravity, or any night-time activities are connected with death, and the occupants of the galaxies. 'If the earth turns around, and the stars turn too, why don't dead people fall off?' 'When my mother meets your mother, will they talk only about us or other things?' For me, mourning the loss of my mother who had died unexpectedly three months before the girls came into my life, it was particularly comforting to picture my own gregarious mum swaddled in a shawl, perched on a star, chatting with the girls' mother.

Having grown up in an institution where most of their friends had lost one parent or both, my daughters view death less as a finality than just one stop on life's journey en route to an afterlife. For children who have seen bereavement at close quarters, they are full of good cheer. With a dramatic slash of podgy fingers across their throats, they indicate that someone or the other has departed from this world. Trying to sleep off a looming headache one afternoon, I hear whispers and jostling. The sheet covering my head is slowly peeled away. 'Are you going to die?' they ask matter-of-factly. Even as I wonder whether to proffer the standard adult lie, 'No, never!' or enter into a philosophical discussion about the transitory nature of life, they zoom to the heart of the matter. 'Who will make our breakfast then? And lunch?' As I reel off the names of potential cooks in their lives – their father, aunt, grandfather, friends, cousins, grandmother – they visibly relax.

My daughters' faith sweeps away doubts and doomsday predictions about the difficulties of bonding with older adopted children. Their optimism and belief in human goodness is irrepressible, despite all that they've been through in their short lives. It takes a while, though, to build lasting trust. They have been through several upheavals already, and it is some time before they can believe that this is real and forever. They stick together; they are a unit – blood sisters. They are often mistaken for twins – close in age, and similar in looks. The illusion of sameness is heightened by the standard issue 'mushroom' haircut of children's institutions, and reinforced by their insistence on wearing the same clothes. They are inseparable, and intensely protective of each other. I am fiercely attacked if I scold one of them, the other immediately springing to her defence, a belligerent pair is better than one. Walking into a room oozing paint from every crevice, or gum splattered on my computer, I am rarely able to find whodunit. Punishments are consequently joint, and they stoically accept collective culpability. If one storms away from the dining table in a sulk, I can be sure that food will be smuggled to her by the other.

A few months later, they begin to bicker. Quarrels erupt about everything. Anything becomes contentious, and we are urged to take sides. Always a test, always the trick question: Who do you love more? Whose painting is better? Saying 'both' is not allowed. Already dealing with two hurricanes whooshing into my life of solitude, the constant high pitched squabbles begin to get to me. Until a psychologist friend drops in and observes, 'Ah good – they've begun to fight. They are more secure, they can loosen their hold on each other, now that you're there to hold them.' I swell with pride, smirking inside: I'm doing a good job of this mothering business.

The complacence is fleeting. Building relationships with five- and six-year-old children is not difficult. But it's easy to forget that they are little people already, with strong personalities, quirks, insecurities and strengths. Other differences are more obvious – the stark cultural, social and class divides. But these are the less consequential differences that people harp on, often making non-issues seem larger than they need to. 'Are they your *real* children?' I am asked. As real as children can ever be, I answer, to their dissatisfaction. Others say with envy, 'Oh, so you skipped the years of sleepless nights and washing nappies.' Grandparents, aunts and uncles, cousins and nieces and nephews embrace them unreservedly, delighted to have children around when those of my contemporaries have grown up and sallied forth into the world with blissful teenage indifference. The girls' generous affection is contagious, their enthusiasm for meeting people unfailing. Despite the insecurity of the first few years of life, they are open and trusting for the most part.

But abandonment and rejection hang like a very fine mist, sometimes blowing away, at others forming dark clouds. Some would argue, including my psychoanalytically inclined husband, that the feeling of abandonment is almost inherent to the human condition: 'Everyone feels abandoned at a psychic level,' I am told. But for children whose biological parents have died or left them with distant family members or institutions, being dumped and passed on from one reluctant relative to the other is a stark reality. It is one that permeates their being in ways that cannot even be imagined. For girls, being unwanted is the default setting, it would seem. But for adopted girls, ironically, loss and rejection from one side and being warmly embraced from the other go almost hand in hand. With the knowledge of having been cast off by their biological families, they are enveloped, soon after, by the deep desire of adoptive parents to nurture. Indeed, adoptive parents live with their yearning for children for many years before it can become a reality.

For adoption and foster parenthood is by no means easy. Adoptive parents have to furnish all manner of proof that they are worthy parents, and prospective single parents, especially single men have an uphill task convincing agencies of their worthiness as parents, which is gauged by income, assets, and 'stability' of relationships. Equal rights and access to adoption for openly lesbian, gay or transgender individuals are not even on the horizon. Inter-country adoptions are tangled in miles of red tape, and laws about adopting more than one child of the same sex have only recently begun to be reviewed and amended. Undoubtedly, there is a flourishing illegal trade in babies and children, and poverty is often a factor pushing families to relinquish their children, not always with their consent. Stories abound of impoverished parents sending their children to 'schools' only to find, a few months later, that they had been given in adoption to a family outside the country. Yet, the tightening of procedures is not always in the best interests of the children or genuine parents. It is a moot point as to how many child traffickers or traders in babies are deterred by the increased bureaucracy. For children with special needs, every extra day in an institution hardens physical, emotional or academic challenges, making any remedial interventions that much more difficult.

The complicated application process, reams of paperwork and then the long wait is akin to a pregnancy in terms of putting things on hold, not making major plans for the future, and the high anticipation. Yet, like childbirth, nothing prepares you for the rush of emotion that accompanies the early days of your children coming home. The first moment of setting eyes on each other is profound. With five- and six-year-olds, there is full awareness that these adults are your parents from now on, and for us, the first introductions, the shy smiles, the tentative hugs, are frozen moments in time. There is a wary acceptance from the start. I soon learn what is treated casually and what is not. If they are not picked up exactly on time from school or day care, they panic. Hanging out of the gates, pigtails askew, anxiety is writ large on their little faces. They have too often been left behind in places where no one came to pick them up ever again. 'Attachment', that much talked about concept is on trial here. I try not to push, not to impose fairy tale endings; trying to allow them an 'exit route' until they no longer feel the need for one.

My tough little elder daughter has a bag packed. Ready to go whenever the going gets tough. She squirrels away goodies in her bag, 'just in case'. There are extra hair clips, toffees and biscuits for her friends in the 'hostel'. She tucks away her favourite skirt, her best-loved bangles. She also includes a set for her sister. Because they have to leave together when 'this' mother is not very nice to them and insists that they finish their dinner before they can have ice cream. But her younger sister wants to stay. Huge fight ensues. 'Ok, *I'm* going back,' declares the elder, and storms out of the house, red bag in tow. The younger one is scared, tears streaming: she waits to see what happens next. 'I want to stay with you, but I want her to stay too,' she sobs. The first time it happens, I follow my instinct, and rush out of the house, dragging the little one along. It's dusk. The winter night is about to make its dramatic descent. At the end of the long, narrow lane I spot a red bag with a forlorn figure perched on it, thin shoulders trembling with the cold. Waiting. Hearing our running footsteps, she turns and flings herself into my arms, clings to me. Wordlessly, we trudge home, wrung out.

The bag is unpacked in silence. There are days when

she begins to fill it up again. Over time, the packing gets less furious, sometimes reduced to a small plastic carry bag. And after some time, it's gone. Now the packing of the red bag is joyous, for vacations. She smiles ruefully when she remembers the fury with which she wanted to get away.

The fantasy of the 'better' mother is not unique to adopted children. Who doesn't remember childhood days when you were convinced that your mother was a stepmother and you simply had to get away to find your 'real' one? This search for the 'model' mother, boyfriend, lover or girlfriend never ends. It's tempting to believe that there is that perfect someone out there, who will love you no matter what. And who doesn't want to set off in search of that one person? Knowing their own parents were dead, our kids had fantasies of different kinds – of being taken in by the perfect parents who would ply them with toys and unlimited supplies of chocolate, never scold them or make them do homework.

And often, one is tempted to do just that, or buy affection out of desperation. Children are so eminently bribe-able, after all – it takes so little to delight them. In a desire to bond, especially in the beginning, it is easier to give, far more difficult to withhold. In the anxiety to make up for previous deprivation – of food, clothes, toys, love, books, learning – filling the gaps too quickly and with too much, can overwhelm the child, akin to a hot chocolate fudge after a week of starvation. Delicious, but the tummy doth protest!

The parent-child relationship template usually rests in large part on dependence and unconditional love. Yet, if the child enters the relationship not as a wholly dependent and vulnerable infant, but as an autonomous individual who is reasonably self-sufficient, it opens the way for a complex give-and-take right from the start. The temptation to 'do everything' for the child, while possibly reassuring, might actually erode autonomy and tilt the power balance in favour of the adult. After all, it is all too easy to love helpless babies and children. The power differential being rather prominent when you enter the parent role at a later stage in the child's life, is a reality check of sorts about the responsible wielding of authority.

One is constantly reminded of the imbalance in the parent-child relationship, much of it predicated on inequities that I fought against as a feminist activist: wealth; access to resources; articulation; superior strength and (in the beginning at least), better skills at manipulation. When the injustice of it is flung back in your face, the balance tilts, often for the better, giving the child a fairer chance in the equation. After a particularly bitter squabble about a very serious matter – whether they should wash their hair that day or the next – my unyielding tyranny is exposed. 'Get lost,' I yell. 'No! We *won't* get lost,' two pairs of heels are dug in. 'If you want, *you* go. This is *our* home, and we're staying here.' I rejoice. Acceptance! I joyously call up my husband, to tell him about their assertion, just two months after they've come: this is *their* home too. A little bewildered over this sudden change of mood, they ask, puzzled, 'So do we wash our hair today or tomorrow?' Back to fundamental questions.

They bring you back to the basics all right. During a

particularly turbulent political period we have no choice
but to make our way across a disturbed land. After a bumpy
five-hour drive during which both kids wanted to pee and
throw up every half hour, we change from bullock carts to
tongas and then cycle rickshaws. Braving the intense mid-
day heat, they scream with delight 'Yay!' The journey is not
tiresome anymore, and we proceed to spot cattle egrets and
ducks in the paddy fields, waving to children paddling in
the streams.

Journeys are magical moments. In buses, we lurch along
pot-holed paths with stupendous views of the mountains,
sucking candy, trying to keep nausea at bay. But co-
passengers are incredibly goodnatured about children
puking over them, clucking in sympathy and sharing the
little black plastic puke bags that characterise bus journeys
in the mountains. We spend leisurely days trekking among
the mightiest peaks in the world, the highest and most
barren cold deserts, the girls chasing sheep and helping to
bathe baby yaks. We stand on the shores of the Arabian Sea,
waves lapping our feet, watch the sun rise over the Bay
of Bengal. Long train journeys across the Subcontinent are
wondrous days in limbo, eating, playing cards, sleeping and
staring out the window. We love where we're coming from,
we're excited about where we're going. And we enjoy the
ride in between.

ANDROMEDA NEBULA is a writer and mother being raised by two
superstars.

Name: Amba Dalmia
Dates: May 19, 1980 – November 19, 2001

MANJU KAPUR

I was 53 when my daughter died.

Even now I do not think I can describe the endless night of November 18th, the visit to the hospital, the return home, the hours that passed, the collective silence of relatives as they gathered in our drawing room.

I remember a frantic burning itch unfurling beneath my skin. For weeks no salve, no ointment, no ice, no heat made any difference.

My reproductive system shut down, this time for good. A hazy disbelief shrouded everything; my mind was doing its best to bar the outside world entry.

The years ahead lay heavy on my heart. I saw myself being pushed down the desolate trajectory of my life – without joy, without hope, each day as bleak as the one before.

So far as I was concerned all the children of the world should die, die at the height of their youth and beauty, die with their lives ahead of them, die and leave their parents grieving, even as I was grieving.

Every morning I opened the newspaper onto the obituary page, to examine the only item that interested me, the death of the young. Ghoulishly, I devoured confirmation that I was not alone.

Although this did nothing to ease my sorrow, I persisted in searching for dead children. Suffering had made me a monster.

Through the day the only pleasure I could anticipate were the sleeping pills at night. My continuing existence tore at me. I, the old parent, inhabiting the minutes, the hours that rightfully belonged to the next generation.

I had failed in my most basic duty: I had not been able to protect my daughter.

You don't let your child go out in unsafe situations. And on that particular night of November 18, 2001 she was unsafe enough to die.

⁕

When I returned to work after two months [I taught in a college], it was with the slow painful walk of a cripple. My words came with difficulty, each lecture presented hurdles I stumbled over.

She had been the same age as these milling students, students walking, eating, studying, secure that to live was their birthright.

What did they know about birthrights? They who looked at me with large tender eyes, they whose gaze I avoided while walking stiff-faced down corridors.

In the staff room, I spent my time staring dully out of the window, my back resolute against sympathy aimed in my direction.

Stay away from me.

I resent your kindness, your determined advance upon my space, anything you say that expresses solidarity, the slightest reference to what happened.

I wished to have nothing to do with the social face of grief.

From time to time I recall with shame the condolence visits I had once paid. How useless I was on those occasions; I with the fixed smile, the trite sympathy, the fearful, there-but-for-the-grace-of-God-go-I feeling in my heart. I had gone in the service of you-are-not-alone but now I understood how much bereavement isolates, and how little difference any interaction makes.

The companionship I sought was of fellow sufferers. You, I will listen to. I respect you, your pain, your endurance, your survival.

One mother: The day you come home from the funeral, the first time you put food into your mouth, that is the moment you have decided to live.

I stare at the black and white portrait of her daughter. The face in three-quarter profile, the wide open smile. I used to call her teeth piano keys, she said.

Piano keys. Nice image. We smile painfully.

It has been two years since her daughter died. She was thirty-three. [Twelves years older than our daughter. Twelve more years of life.]

In some ways the second year is harder, she continued. By then it has sunk in, well and truly sunk in.

Oh. So there was all of that to look forward to.

We were meeting in a church. She had put out a notice announcing a support group for parents in mourning.

Someone had told us about it and here we were. The only attendees.

The woman was a counsellor.

In India perhaps this kind of gathering will not be so successful, she observed. People already have family, friends whom they rely on. But I was part of such a group in the US and it really helped. [Her daughter had died in an American hospital.]

We talk about marriage break-ups. Couples separate – they can't take the burden of grief – their own and their partner's. They want to get on with life.

It is not as though I am averse to getting on. I only wonder how you can do it when your spirits are so weighed down you cannot move. And what was the use of splitting up with your partner? For who else in the world could this particular loss be as significant?

❊

Some time after the event, I walk hesitatingly to my study. Hesitation because with each step I move towards a life that no longer contains her and that wrongs every moment.

On the way I notice that the gladioli I had planted earlier have begun to bloom. The gay red tips hurt me with their insouciance.

It shows how stupid I have become. I feel personally aggrieved by the way everything continues. I long for a day when flowers can flourish, birds can sing and I not be offended.

I unlock my study door and enter.

I stare at my computer, squat black, the morning light

reflected off its thick layer of dust. How can I do the same things when everything is changed? It seems morally reprehensible.

The before time, the after time.

There are some things we never do again. I have never since stuck a photo in an album, never put mehndi on my hands. My husband stopped pursuing his development plans, abandoning a project that had been his dream for over 20 years. There are places we don't visit because they are associated with her, songs we don't listen to, books we don't open, drawers that remain shut. Unbeknownst to anybody, we continue with our pointless statements.

I turn the machine on and dredge up the novel I am working on. I scroll down page after page. I can barely understand what I have written, let alone relate to the characters. I feel as weak before the narrative as a baby in a grown-up world.

I close the file.

Writing had once meant a lot to me, and now I wonder whether this too has collapsed along with so much else. My hands move over the keys. Uncertainly, I begin to jot down a bit of what I have been going through.

It is useless. Words cannot do justice to what I feel. I switch the computer off. In the now blank screen I can see my dim reflection. The reflection of a 53-year-old woman.

I make a list of authors who have lost their children:

William Shakespeare, Rabindranath Tagore, Roald Dahl, Mary Shelley, Goethe, Isabel Allende, Carlos Fuentes, J.M. Coetzee, Mridula Garg.

This is a list I find soothing. I cling to Shakespeare &

Co and continue switching on my computer and gazing at the screen.

❦

Two women:

Indu Jain.

We are related, Indu Bhabhi and I.

A few months earlier she lost her daughter in a helicopter crash. Her husband and grandson are also dead.

The point about Indu Bhabhi is not the number of deaths in her family but how she looks.

All her life she has been a seeker. Her skin glows, her face is youthful, her whole demeanor suffused with joy. Her gurus and her spiritual practice are the source of her strength.

She invites us to her house. There she is sitting on a divan dressed in orange robes. When she talks it is of the delusions of the mind, when she offers consolation it is through realising its strength.

I come home feeling uplifted but soon my sad reality hits me and I am back to where I started.

No matter how long it takes, I want to look like Indu Bhabhi.

Anu Aga.

Within fourteen months, Anu Aga lost both her son and husband. Though this has rendered her completely alone at both home and business, she emanates a beautiful self-sufficiency. A little digging and I find she meditates. She refers to her Vipassana retreat.

I choose these women as my role models.

※※

Essential to the spiritual practices I have been studying is the doctrine of karma. Tentatively I suggest to my family that in karma might lie the answer as to why she had to die so suddenly at the age of 21.

My younger daughter has a sharp nose for intellectual honesty. So now its karma? she demands.

Me: Yes.

YD: Don't you think that's a bit convenient?

Me: Perhaps.

YD: Perhaps? You never believed in the stuff before, how can you suddenly turn to it?

Me: It has its uses.

YD: Of course it has its uses. But karma is also used to manipulate, you know that. Remember what Marx said?

She finds me the quotation: Religion is the sigh of the oppressed creature, the heart of a heartless world… It is the opium of the people. The abolition of religion as illusory happiness… is required for their real happiness.

YD: See? It is part of needing illusions.

Me: I know, I know. But if I believe that it was her karma to die and mine to suffer, it just makes things better. If it was destined, there was nothing I could have done to avoid it. It may be false comfort, but still it provides some reason – and therefore some relief.

YD stares at me. I can see I make no sense. In addition to her own sorrow she has to deal with her parents falling apart.

And of course, we cannot think alike on this one. She cannot – and should not – believe in karma. At the beginning of her life to be imbued with these fatalistic notions? No.

Though our loss is common our way of grieving is not. In the family all of us have responded differently, according to our temperaments, our emotional registers, our ages, and our relationship to the girl. Though we are tender towards each other, we are as essentially divided as it is possible for people living under one roof to be.

❦

Six months pass. Teaching is over for the year. I am now free to go to a ten-day Vipassana retreat in Dehradun, to an ashram that overlooks a dry stony riverbed.

For ten days I will not speak. I will get up at 4am to spend ten hours meditating. I will eat two meals in mindful silence. I will not be allowed to read.

Do I wish to look into myself quite so much? And not read?

But if I want some way out of this stupefying wretchedness I have no choice. In Buddhism happiness is a spiritual goal. I yearn for that happiness, that freedom from emotional maelstroms.

Hour after hour in the meditation hall. We do not move. Backs straight, cross-legged on specially designed cushions.

The men and women occupy opposite sides. There is no fan. It is very quiet.

I sit and I sit.

Angry as I am, I decide to be angry with the leaders of our meditation. It is all very well for them to look so tranquil. I'd like to see them maintain that calm in the face of losing a child, I just would.

I seek a private interview with the woman leader, I tell her about my daughter. She listens attentively before giving me the one piece of information that has any relevance, the death of her son in his early twenties.

I am duly chastened. There is suffering everywhere, in how many ways does this need to be brought home to me?

I resume my meditation and do what I am supposed to do, which is look inside. I have tried to avoid this, but when you are seated for ten hours, in the silence that determined non-movement brings, you can do nothing else.

Images of my daughter appear. Her gaze is fixed on me, but her look is solemn. Wordlessly she climbs into my lap. I wrap my arms around her, straining her slight young body against my old heavy one. I cry and cry, you didn't say goodbye, you didn't tell me you were going. Her head is against my shoulder, her own arms folded around my neck. Then she disengages herself, unzips a tent placed in the middle of my heart, bends down to enter it and from the outside I see the zip slowly travelling up as the flaps shut. The tent is light blue, her track suit is pale pink as are her neat little canvas shoes.

This was her farewell. My face is damp, my palla wet with snot and tears. I would see her twice more in dreams. Then never again.

I left the Vipassana centre convinced of the efficacy of meditation. This indeed was the route to non-suffering. The ten-day retreat had put a tiny distance between my grief and me and I was determined to continue. Both morning and night I meditated for one hour. But my mind – as is the nature of minds – proved resistant to the slightest discipline. The same one thing swum round and round and, by the time the year was out, I had stopped meditating.

***

That summer N and I fly down to Pondicherry. The Aurobindo Ashram is one of the many places we visit in search of some balm to soothe our torment. We meet a senior teacher there. In shorts and a T-shirt he appears happy, contented, calm and serene.

He has given up his life in Delhi – a decision he spent eight months thinking about – to join his guru in the Ashram. He helps to run the place.

Taking in his demeanour, I too have this wild desire to flee Delhi. The Aurobindo Ashram will be my future home.

But of course it is not the place, is it? No place can free you from your suffering. Not a single place in the entire world.

As he shows us around, we tell him our story, one we have told many times. What can anyone tell us that will make the pain recede? At some level I feel our quest is hopeless, yet we are driven on.

The man begins to describe the mind. A mad monkey, a mad, sick, crazed on drugs, frenetic, jumping wildly from tree to tree monkey.

It is a favourite analogy this one – the similarity between the mind and a monkey, one I was to come across many times. The responsibility of controlling the monkey was ours. We and we alone had the power to remove our suffering.

We ask desultory questions. After a point he says you just have to experience it. Words cannot make you feel a spiritual reality.

It is December – 13 months since Amba died. I am sitting in the garden.

A nephew is getting married. With ceremonies lasting one week it promises to be the event of the year. It is one of the first weddings of this generation in our family and there is much excitement.

Clothes, jewellery, parties, gossip, activity, activity, activity.

Amba would have been in the centre of such things. She adored company and company adored her. She loved interacting with people, intuitively relating to them at all levels. Her visitors never stopped coming, her phone never stopped ringing, her fingers never stopped tapping out the hundreds of numbers she knew by heart. I am a people person she would say from time to time.

Her eyes were shaped like gleaming almonds. Her fingers were long and slender, so was her neck. She had a little mole at the tip of her nose; a mole that she wanted removed.

I sit among the growing flowers and count the days left to the wedding. But what was the use? This one over, there would be others. Her cousins, her friends, and we invited to them all. What else could anyone do? They wanted to remember – we wanted them to remember. We were what was left of her. We had to be involved.

I am 54 now. How much longer did I have left to live?

To go to sleep and never get up – a consummation devoutly to be wished.

Ameeta, my sister-in-law's friend, wanders by.

How are you, Manju?

Fine is a word that tastes of ashes in my mouth.

I want to die, I reply.

She sits down to look at me with the earnest sympathetic gaze I now attract. It is a look I hate – don't pity me – but mixed with my resistance is a sense of my own dreadful isolation. Nobody can talk to me – what is there to say? Nobody can talk of anything else – I'm not interested.

Why, Manju?

No answer. I am a dog chasing its tail, trapped in a cycle of desolation.

Why don't you try this Buddhism I practise? It does make a difference, I promise. What do you have to lose?

Always this statement hovering over everything I refused to try. What did I have to lose?

This was how I was introduced to the Soka Gakkai and chanting Nam myoho renge kyo.

Imagine things you want, commanded Ameeta.

My belief in karma though stronger than before was not doing an adequate job in enabling me to come to terms with what had happened. Tranquility, acceptance? Nowhere on the horizon.

Despite myself there were things that I wanted. After all I was still living.

A family that was healed.

A husband to recover fully from the cardiac arrest a year of relentless grief had brought on.

For now this was enough.

Most forms of Buddhism actively deal with suffering. The BSG was the structure that propped me up – day after day, with person after person coming to visit me, chant with me, talk to me.

It is incompatible to want things and simultaneously wish yourself dead. In a shift so tiny it was imperceptible, the hope I thought had disappeared forever, glimmered fitfully. Drops of water falling on a stone. Another favourite analogy implying that eventually you will get there.

So, with crutch in hand, I went on.

Karma, karma, her karma, my karma.

As I chanted I gradually stopped feeling like a victim. I stopped asking why me? Why her?

It's been over ten years now. Ten years – with all my subsequent life wrapped like a pearl around this lacerating grain of sand.

The way I think is now deeply influenced by what I practise. Every day, day in and day out for years together I have tried to change myself into a person who possesses the Buddhist virtues of wisdom, courage and compassion. A person who recognises in the depths of her being that you cannot hang onto anything, not even your children. That if you manage to accept this basic fact you will not feel so violated.

The teacher at Aurobindo Ashram was right: a spiritual journey is difficult to explain in words. Words seem tired, old, self-evident, obvious and simple, even while embodying precepts almost impossible to follow.

✤

Whenever I hear of parents whose children have died (or worse, committed suicide) I think of the long, long road ahead of them. I want to rush out and hold their hands, assure them that their darkness will lift, that though their lives have changed irrevocably, they will be able to experience light again, a different light from the one they thought they would live in earlier, but light nonetheless.

I want to present a smiling face. See, this happened to me. It happened, I thought nobody could help, but that was not true. I was helped, by many, many – even though it did not feel like help at the time. It felt like wanton intrusion into my misery.

I will tell them how angry I was. My life had been desecrated. The only thing I yearned for was that the clock should turn back, and I live in the blessed time before. And the only people I wanted to meet were those who had lost their children.

They must know they are not alone. There are others. And there will continue to be others.

Manju Kapur taught English literature in Miranda House for over 25 years. Her novel *Difficult Daughters* won the Commonwealth Prize for best first novel, Eurasia region in 1998. She is also the author of *A Married Woman* (2002), *Home* (2006) [shortlisted for the Hutch-Crossword Prize], and *The Immigrant* (2008) [shortlisted for the India Plaza Golden Quill Award and the DSC Prize of South Asian Literature]. Her work has been translated into German, Portuguese, Italian, Spanish, Dutch, Hebrew, Marathi and Hindi. Her latest novel, *Custody* (2011), deals extensively with children.

Portrait of the Mother as a Chair

MRIDULA KOSHY

Vani's forearm protested the baby's hard skull as it rotated from her. The mouth made strangled sounds that were not sounds of rotation. The sense of those sounds was clear. Straining from the shoulder, the body attempted to follow the face that was done turning away. Momentarily exhausted, the baby lay face up in Vani's arms. Her eyes found Vani's. This contact was not to be borne. The baby jerked her head as if to fling it from her thin neck. If allowed to, Padma would finish the work of turning her back to Vani. Vani moved to gather Padma back to her. The baby bottle she had fought free from Padma was slippery with milk, the hole in the nipple torn and leaking. Vani needed to put the bottle down, but not on the bed where she was seated. The moment's indecision left her facing the flattened back of the baby's head, with the round of yellow skin visible through the broken off hair, the hair appearing to have been scrubbed away with a scouring pad.

There had been similar dark marks on Suresh's neck when he was new – indication of past bouts with scabies. The white scurf of infancy still clinging in crusty patches to Padma's eighteen-month-old scalp was only mildly disgusting to Vani.

The ayah had instructed Vani to scratch it off. Vani had told the ayah she knew what she needed to do.

Vani placed the bottle carefully upright on the bed and brought her hand to the head. Padma pulling away, harder still, tumbled from her arms, face down onto the bed. Vani was immediately penitent. She picked the baby up; rearranging the long limbs, she laid Padma onto her lap. She brought the bottle into Padma's line of vision. Using it as bait, she coaxed the face toward her. Eye contact churned the air between them. She made herself smile, she offered the nipple. The mouth opened, grasped the nipple. Cautious swallowing sounds broke the silence. The eyes clenched themselves shut. Hands reached for the bottle. Vani allowed that they could remain, their touch was light. And with each pull of the mouth at the torn nipple, the hands exerted their pull. The bottle slipped bit by glass and resistant bit from Vani. Vani pulled back. The two agreed only on the need for silence.

The door opened. It was Manoj. He looked in and frowned then returned to the smile with which he was attempting to coax their son in the door.

'Shunu,' he used Suresh's baby name. 'Come see, the baby is awake. Even I haven't seen the baby awake. Look, Mummy is feeding the baby.'

Suresh looked in the room from behind his father. His eyes said, don't want to see, but he came in compliantly enough. He was wearing rather grubby Friday whites, the teeth of the belt buckle half grasped the red belt; an un-looped length of it pulled out from him, outlining a yet invisible additional belly.

'Come sit,' Vani patted to indicate where he should sit

on the bed, to indicate welcome. She hadn't seen him since the previous Saturday when she had left to bring the baby home. She got ready a kiss for him.

He wore his shy look. It was as likely a look of boredom and even hostility. But it was accepted in the family as his look of shyness; she had led the charge on that front, and with such force that even as she remained unconvinced, everyone else had long given way.

Up close he was huge to her. This hugeness alone would have sufficed as hostility. How quickly he was growing. Bloating. She felt herself suffocating. She was simultaneously grateful to see him so huge.

'You've gotten so big. Look at your big brother, Padma. Look, he is such a big boy.' Suresh looked pained. She landed the kiss on his cheek. He did not wipe it away. There was sweat from his cheek on her lips.

Vani turned to Manoj. 'You know what your sister said to me before? She said as soon as I returned with Padma I would see that Suresh was suddenly so much bigger. And see, she was right. Shunu, your Prabha aunty predicted it.'

'Prabha is acting like Big-Mummy; she's repeating what Big-Mummy would have said. Whenever I returned from summer in Hyderabad, hell even from two days anywhere, it was always, Oh you've gotten so big. I would have gladly shrunk just to get her to stop all the kissing. And the pinching.' He winked at Suresh. 'You've gotten so big, so huge, so handsome etcetera, etcetera.'

'What etcetera, etcetera? It's not talk. Shunu is a big boy. And handsome.' Vani put a hand on her cheek. It felt hot. She wiped her lips.

'Well of course Suresh is a big boy now. Has to be. He has additional responsibilities. Big brother now. You can help your mother. Let him take the bottle and hold it for the baby.'

'That's not what Prabha was saying. It isn't like the elder one has more responsibilities and that makes them grow or something. She said when she had Gauri, Ashish turned into a giant. Immediately. It was in her eyes he turned into a giant. Maybe it's something that happens to mothers only, not to fathers. It happened to her with Ashish.'

'What nonsense. How could Ashish turn into a giant? Ashish was only two when Gauri was born.'

Vani slid over on the bed and picking one of Padma's feet from where it dangled off her lap she brought it to Suresh's touch. He laid a finger on the foot. Then dragged it back and forth on the foot. Padma accepted this.

Wasn't this what Prabha had told her to expect? Yes, her sister-in-law, bearer of Ashish and Gauri had told her this would happen to her. 'To everyone else he'll actually be the same he ever was. But to you he will seem huge because the baby will be so tiny, so pretty, so sweet, you'll see. Ashish became a giant. I didn't even want to go near him after that. Gauri was so perfect compared to him. It took me a little while to get used to Ashish again.'

Later on, Prabha had added, 'After a few weeks of not sleeping at night the baby won't be so perfect, and naturally I didn't continue to feel like Ashish was a giant. But at the time I felt so guilty about it. Don't worry when it happens to you, it's all normal.'

Vani patted her own cheeks. Then she patted Suresh's.

Here she was. And in fact Suresh was huge. She had become one of those mothers who would have to wait for her older child to return to normal size. She could see Prabha had been right. Shunu was huge. Huger than the huge he used to be. And sweaty. And if Padma at nearly a year and a half was no longer the new-born, so tiny, so dainty, so perfect – there was still a huge difference between her and Shunu.

She lamented, 'Your uniform, Shunu. How did you manage to get it so dirty? Look at your shorts, they're coming apart. See Manoj? Splitting at the seam. Don't argue with me. You're going to have to get him two new pairs at the uniform shop.'

'Vani, let Suresh hold the bottle. Come son, you feed the baby.'

What else had Prabha said? 'You won't even want to go near your husband. Of course for you there won't be the endless bleeding and discomfort. Such animals, they won't wait you know. All that stuff people went in for in the past – separate sleeping and returning to your own home for the birth – it was all for good reason. It wasn't just up to the men then.'

'Manoj,' she put entreaty in her voice. 'If it was up to me, we wouldn't have the puja tonight. I haven't seen you and Suresh in almost a week.'

She jiggled Padma in her lap. The milk bottle was done. Suresh was playing with Padma's toes, counting them out loud. Padma was chewing on the nipple. Vani tapped on the bottle. The baby would not give it up. Manoj did not reply. She stole a look at him.

Wasn't it at the puja after she brought Suresh home,

wasn't it then that Prabha said what she said. 'But Vani, didn't they let you choose?'

'When I've been home for a bit, Manoj, we can have the puja then. I need my strength to handle the kind of things that get said. You remember?' She nodded her head in Suresh's direction to indicate why she couldn't spell out for Manoj what he was supposed to remember.

'No, I don't remember. And if you mean that bit from the past with Prabha, you know it's just something that slipped out. I think there's been enough apologizing from everyone about everything that ever happened or didn't happen.'

Vani shrugged. He was right about one thing: there would be no hasty comment made tonight. The family will gather to welcome the new baby, the baby they have not chosen, no more in any case than any one chooses any baby.

Vani didn't really mean her entreaty to put off the puja. She was looking forward to showing the baby off. There's a yellow dress and matching hat waiting in the almarih for the baby. She will give Padma a bath and she will take a long bath herself. They will get dressed. She turned to Suresh,

'You were tiny once, like her.'

'And you used to feed me with a bottle.'

'Yes. I mean no. It wasn't exactly the same. Every baby is different.'

She tugged gently at the bottle. What had Suresh seen from the doorway, hidden away behind Manoj?

'You want to try to hold her? Cross your legs, here, like this and I will lay her on your lap.'

In preparation for the transfer she tugged again at the

bottle. Padma replied by clamping her teeth down on the nipple; mid-air between her and Suresh, the nipple came away with a little pop. Padma screamed as if she had been burnt. Mid-air, Vani retuned her, bucking, to her lap. She returned the bottle to Padma.

'I want to hold her,' Suresh insisted.

'She likes to hold her bottle. It will take time for her to get used to it here. To us.'

'Did I like to hold my bottle too?'

Vani ignored the question. She jerked her knees up and down and Padma began hiccupping in time with the motion.

'Yes. I mean no. All babies like to hold their own bottles. But their mummies have to hold the bottle. Not the babies.'

'So you held my bottle?'

'Yes.'

'Why?'

'It's important to make sure the baby doesn't choke.'

Vani put her hand on Padma's forehead. A hiccup of protest slid the nipple from Padma's mouth. Her mouth grabbed after the nipple, took it and spat it out. Padma tore into another scream.

Manoj stepped into the room. 'Like this,' he said. He picked the baby up and sat her upright on his lap. And as suddenly the distorted features righted themselves, and there was Padma, dry eyes and cheeks, even a small smile in the general direction of the room. Manoj jiggled her on his lap then transferred the baby to Suresh. Suresh took the bottle from Vani and offered it to Padma who settled back in his lap and sucked as if there was indeed something in the bottle.

'She is just like you were, Suresh. You used to like to sit drinking your milk on your mummy's lap, looking out at everything that was happening.'

'Daddy, did I like to look at you?'

'Yes Shunu, you liked to look at me.'

'She likes to look at you too.'

'Yes, Padma likes to look at me.'

'But I was littler than she was.'

'Yes, you were just four months old.'

Sometime after, Manoj left the room. Suresh squirmed to indicate he was done. Vani uncrossed her legs and hung them from the bed. Lifting Padma up by her underarms, she transferred the baby to her lap. She allowed Padma to keep the bottle though she offered her hand under the bottle to prop it up for as long as Padma wanted to continue sucking at it.

'It's not an easy way to hold a baby.'

Suresh leaned against Vani. Sleepy now, his words came slowly. 'Yes, but it's easy for the baby.'

'Yes,' Vani agreed, 'it is easy for the baby.' Wrapping one arm around the baby's chest to keep Padma from sliding from her lap, Vani put the other arm cautiously around Suresh. 'Do you remember, you used to, like Daddy just said, you used to not want to lie down, you also liked to sit up, facing out like Padma?'

He answered her with his own question. 'How did you get her?'

Thinking he was asking her for his story, she began,

'Long time ago, before you were even born, your daddy and I wanted to have a baby very badly. So we kept checking to see if there was a baby in my tummy.'

Vani paused. Afternoon was coming to an end. The only sound in the room was the fan turning. After a while she registered the dishes being washed in the kitchen.

'Then one day we found out our baby – you – were not in my tummy. You were elsewhere. And you meanwhile were checking to see where is your mummy, where is your daddy. We were all searching.'

He interrupted. 'No, I want to know how did you get *her*?'

'Well,' she said 'ever since Big-Mummy died, your daddy and I have been wanting a new baby.'

'Before that when Big-Mummy was still alive, she didn't want you to have a new baby.'

'Oh no. That's not true. Where did you hear that?'

'Nowhere.'

'Nowhere?'

'Before, you wanted a new baby even before, didn't you? But if you went to get a baby before, it would have been a different baby? It wouldn't be this one.'

'Yes. Maybe yes, it would have been a different baby. Not Padma. But the thing is we find the baby that is searching for us. At the right time. At the time we are searching for the baby. That's how we did it with you. So this happened at the right time. See? We have our baby. Padma.'

She begins again and is measured this time. 'It happened that it was after Big-Mummy died that Daddy and I started to think about having another baby. Prabha aunty and

Bobby Uncle decided to move from upstairs. They wanted to have their own house. You know that before you were even born, your Dadaji, your Big-Daddy was also living here, ever since then we have all been a big family. But now it is only the three of us in such a big house. Your daddy and I thought you must be feeling alone and also you must be wanting your own little sister. Your cousin Ashish has Gauri, no? And when Padma is bigger, she will want to play with you. And now you can help me to take care of her.'

'You told me all this already. I want to know how. How did you get her? How do you get a baby if it's not in your tummy for you to have?'

'Oh,' Vani spoke slowly, 'you're asking how. 'How' is like this. If you have so much love for a baby but your tummy cannot make that baby, then God makes that baby for you somewhere else.'

'But how somewhere else?'

'You remember when Prabha aunty was going to have Ashish. You were four years old then. And again just two years ago when she had Gauri. You saw how Ashish and Gauri were in Prabha auntie's tummy. You saw how it became big and round and she had to go to the hospital. Shunu, you know before we became your Mummy and Daddy you were born in another mother's stomach. We've talked about how sometimes the other mother cannot keep her baby. When Prabha aunty was getting ready to have Ashish, remember we saw how her tummy was getting bigger and Ashish was growing inside her and we looked all over the house for your old baby clothes for Ashish to wear and Uncle got a specially made cot for the baby and we had to buy new bottles for him to drink his milk. It happens sometimes a mother can make a baby inside her but she cannot keep him because she doesn't have things to take care of him.'

'Is it because babies come from God?'

'Yes, it's very much because babies come from God.'

'And if sometimes there's a mistake and the baby gets put in the wrong place. Like I was put in the wrong place and then you were waiting for me to come in your tummy and then when I didn't you went to look for me and you found me and that's how.'

'Yes, that's how. As you grow older you will understand better.'

'But if there's one mistake, can there be another?'

'Shunu, there's no mistake. You're my little boy.'

'Yes, but maybe Padma is in the wrong place here, and soon someone else might realise she belongs with them and come looking for her.'

Vani laughed. She gave him a little mock thump on his too prominent belly. He pretended to cave in, pulling into himself the belt buckle that was loose and his belly button that had been showing through the gapped opening of his shirt. She laughed. She kissed the top of his head that butted up into her side, where it hurt her. 'Shunu, you naughty, jealous boy. Your sister is here to stay.' He laughed from inside his caved-in belly.

The family dinner and puja are a long, long ways in the future. And a long, long ways in the future, her sister-in-law's incursion into this happiness. A long, long time after dinner tonight, after the Pundit's, 'This is a powerful child, she pulled you to her', after Prabha's, 'Oh yes, Punditji, our children choose us, we do not choose them,' will come her own conviction, 'She did not choose me,' and only then will this happiness disperse.

And after the end of this happiness, after Prabha, the Pundit, the choosing and not choosing, sometime after everyone has passed the baby from hand to hand, there will be a family portrait. Vani has a yellow dress and matching hat waiting in the almarih for the baby. The dress is yellow but it is also green and she picked it though Manoj would have liked it to have been pink. They'll group themselves around her – her husband will stand on one side, her son on the other and she will be seated with the baby seated on her. And they will, all of them, face out.

MRIDULA KOSHY is the author of *Not Only the Things That Have Happened* (Harper Collins India). Her short story collection, *If It Is Sweet* won the 2009 Shakti Bhatt First Book Prize and was shortlisted for the 2009 Vodafone Crossword Book Award. Koshy would like to take this opportunity to thank Saleem, Akshay and Surya for repeatedly clarifying to her (in 1997, in 2000, in 2004 and every day in between and since) that motherhood is indeed the most intellectually challenging work to be had on the planet, in addition of course to being the most drudgery she has undertaken, ever. All of which Koshy would like to argue is reason to pay her, and other mothers, a salary. Same as any other worker who contributes to the GDP, GNP and let's not forget that most important measure of wellbeing, the general level of lovingness in our world.

The Business of Mothering

SHASHI DESHPANDE

Years back, at an event organised by the feminist publishers Virago for my novel *That Long Silence*, a woman in the audience asked a question, more of Virago than of me: why, when it was a feminist publishing house, did the author's bio-data speak of her father and not of her mother?

The answer, as far as I was concerned, was simple; the bio-data had to do with my novel, it was in the context of me as a writer, in the context of my writing. And therefore, my father, who was a writer, and an intellectual influence on me, had to be mentioned. Whereas, my mother had nothing to do with my writing.

Today, decades later, I would question the question: does feminism mean inflating the importance of mothers beyond what they actually meant in our lives? Does feminism, in other words, mean going beyond the truth to right the balance?

And today I also correct myself: my mother did influence me, there's no way I can deny that. It was from my mother that I learnt what it is to be a woman, it was from her that I got my idea of a family, because my father, essentially a loner, was estranged from his own family. And my mother did have a connection with my writing, because it was from her that I got stories of women. She often spoke to us about her large, joint family, she gave us stories of women in the family: an aunt of hers, widowed in early childhood and living the hard, austere life of a widow after that. Bringing up all the motherless children whose mothers died young. Of another aunt who, when widowed, was saved from having her head shaved because her brother stood up against it. She told us about yet another aunt, an unusually intelligent woman, who had a child each year, who hated it and who, as she had predicted, finally died in childbirth. These women came back to me later when I began writing, their stories kick-started my own writing, they shaped me into becoming the kind of writer I was to be. My first novel *Roots and Shadows*, came, in fact, out of my mother's family, out of their large house, the *wada*, which was such an intrinsic part of my childhood.

Undeniably, our ideas of motherhood come from our mothers and very often they are the standard by which we judge ourselves as mothers. But as a child I was disobedient, argumentative and rebellious, always questioning and rejecting my mother's statements and her authority. Yet some of the things she said about motherhood stayed like burrs in my mind for years, ideas that, as I grew older, I found myself weighing and judging. Ideas like a mother's love being absolute and unconditional. (And yet I saw how it could be withdrawn, how conditional it could often be.) The idea that mothers are self-sacrificing and will give up everything for their children. (Children, I realised, take this for granted and rarely remember the sacrifices until later in life.) That motherhood is instinctive, and deeply ingrained in all women. And therefore, as soon as the child is born, the mother gets all the qualities of motherhood. And that motherhood is the greatest and the most noble thing in the world; to be without a mother is the biggest tragedy for a child. (My mother had lost her mother at a very tender age: I now understand why motherhood meant so much to her.)

But these ideas were not just my mother's. They were all around me, floating in the air, ideas which I absorbed, it seems, through a process of osmosis. Ideas masquerading as the truths about mothers and motherhood. I had to become a mother myself to realise that there is no single truth about motherhood. There are various truths, according to the way we see it; I had to find out my own truths about motherhood.

Gradually I realised that there were things no one spoke about and that you have to learn these from your own experience. Like the pain I suffered when giving birth, a monstrous pain in which I felt trapped. What was also a revelation to me was the confusion at having suddenly become responsible for this tiny squalling human. I had not expected this, I was not ready for it. I had been made to feel that becoming a mother was a beautiful experience, a blissful one. (Remember the ads that show a beautiful young woman with a look of rapture on her face, gently caressing her swollen abdomen?) Instead, there was bewilderment. And fear, fear which began when I felt the baby's head lolling on the frail neck, which, it seemed, might snap at any moment. Fear when I saw the dip of the fontanelle in the tiny skull, when I felt the throbbing pulse just under the thin skin; I was terrified at the vulnerability of the baby. There were other fears too, the fear of dying and leaving the baby motherless.

If these fears were difficult to articulate, it was even harder to speak of the lowness of spirits which came upon me now and then. As a mother of a healthy baby, being looked after by my mother, I was supposed to feel on top of the world. Why, then, did I feel this way? Was I an abnormal mother? Years later I read Sylvia Plath's words in a letter to her mother, (the last letter she wrote before she killed herself): '*To be catapulted from the cowlike happiness of maternity into loneliness and grim problems is no fun.*' But I was not lonely and had no problems, certainly none as grim as hers. What was it then?

Looking back, I think that what really overwhelmed me was the way my entire life had been taken away from me by the baby and his needs. There was no space left for anything else. I had always wanted to be free of others' demands, I had shied away from responsibility. Now I was chained to this little bit of humanity. There was nothing else in my life; the world had receded, those years are a blank. I, who had read incessantly, now had no time to read even the newspaper. Books, movies, events passed me by. I remember my sister and her husband coming home to wish my husband on his birthday. 'Birthday?' I asked, bleary-eyed with lack of sleep, exhausted with looking after a baby who did not know that the night was for sleeping and an active child of three. Nothing had prepared me for this.

But time, as always, works its magic. And these, my deepest fears. were banished to the dark corners of my being once the infants became toddlers and then children, who ran, laughed, played, fought, argued. Round-the-clock care was no longer required. Soon the children became aware of their own burgeoning selves, they resisted authority, they were sassy and disobedient.

The world came back to me and I knew that I needed to get away for at least a few hours a day, I needed to do something that had nothing to do with this constant, ceaseless caring, I needed to wake up my intellectual self which seemed to have got lost in endless repetitive tasks, in the constant emotional churning. Fearfully, I joined a journalism course. Fearful, because I wondered whether I could leave the children even for a few hours, wondered whether I could cope with any intellectual activity. Wasn't it Bernard Shaw who had said that a woman loses her intellectual capacity when she becomes a mother? It reassured me that I did very well. But it was not easy. It was hard to get away from the children for the three or four hours for my classes. I felt guilty, I wondered whether it was worth it. I remember trying to write my thesis, an imperative before getting the diploma, while my younger son, less than three then, kept banging at the door calling out for me.

'Motherhood means being instantly interruptible, responsive, responsible. Children need you now.'

Tillie Olsen's statement in *Silences*. A book I read a little later and which went straight to my heart. A book which gives a bleak, a slightly alarming picture. An exaggerated picture, I think, when I read it now. But perhaps it had to be the way it was, considering the time when it was written, the 1960s, when feminism suddenly made its presence felt, when it was clamouring to be taken seriously. Olsen's book speaks of all kinds of silences, especially of writers' silences, more especially of writer-mothers' silences. Until recently, she says, all distinguished achievement has come from childless women, because it was impossible to combine motherhood with work. Tillie Olsen gives a long list of childless women writers, from Jane Austen to Virginia Woolf, from Iris Murdoch to Joyce Carol Oates. Yes, pregnancy and child-rearing, 'the business of mothering' as Jane Austen called it, took years – no, *decades* – of a woman's life. And it drained her, made her unable to do any other work. When Jane Austen heard of a niece's second or third pregnancy in as many years of marriage, she called her 'Poor Animal,' adding, 'she will be worn out before she is thirty.' Jane Austen had every right to dread childbearing; three of her sisters-in-law died in childbirth leaving behind a large family of motherless children.

But those were the days before contraception, a time when women went on having children until menopause, or until they died. Now, it is no longer an either/or situation; contraception makes sure that you can have just as many children as you choose, that you can space your children according to your needs. It means that a woman can go back to her work after the first few years of the children's life – like I did, like many women did and continue to do. But does this mean that we are better mothers? That we can give better and more care to the children because there are fewer of them? Or does it mean that children get too much attention, that children are lonely? Hard to find the truth. My children are my success, a young woman, who had been a single parent, told me. A rare mother, a rare statement. Most of us agonise: have I been a good mother? Have I given the children what they needed? It doesn't help that there is this ideal of motherhood floating around us, this idea that there is something called the perfect mother. Even more frightening is the thought that a mother makes or mars her children. It is a huge burden to carry.

Where does this idea of a perfect mother come from? From myths? But, when I revisited them, I found to my surprise, that most of the women in the myths are more wives than mothers. Sita is mostly wife, her motherhood takes place backstage, so to say. Draupadi, too, is only wife almost through the Mahabharata; her motherhood comes to the fore only when her sons die. And Savitri, of course, is totally wife. It seems to me that wifehood needed to be emphasised, because it did not come instinctively like motherhood does. Women had to be told what being a good wife meant, they had to be kept sternly on that path through these examples. Motherhood need not be preached; it doesn't have to be consciously taught.

Yet, there is more cant surrounding motherhood than any other subject, except perhaps romantic love. Thankfully, writers see things more clearly, good writers go past the cant and the stereotypes. And therefore, literature can and does give us a fairly clear picture of mothers and motherhood, literature gives us all kinds of mothers. Dickens has Mrs Nickleby, a silly mother, Mrs Jellyby in *Bleak House*, the neglectful mother, Mrs Clennam, Arthur Clennam's mother in *Little Dorrit*, the cruel mother, David Copperfield's mother, a weak gentle creature who cannot protect her son from her cruel dominating husband. (My own favourite is Mrs Wilfer in *Our Mutual Friend*, the stately domineering woman who terrifies her husband, but whose daughters see through her and are not daunted by her.) Yet when it comes to his heroines, Dickens always presents them as wonderful mothers, he ends the story with a glimpse of the heroine, her little children clustered round her. Heroines, good women, have necessarily to be good mothers. Perhaps, as Sudhir Kakkar says, men have a tendency to canonise their mothers; the good mother picture, he says, is a male construct.

I am not sure this is entirely true, but undoubtedly women are more practical and matter-of-fact about motherhood. Jane Austen, for example, has Mrs Bennet, the stupid vulgar mother. And there's Mary, Anne Elliott's sister in *Persuasion*, who has no idea how to deal with her children. Fanny Price's mother in *Mansfield Park*, who neglects and ignores her brood of children, doting only on her eldest, William, openly showing her partiality. In Gauri Deshpande's Marathi novel, *Nirgathi*, the mother–child relationship is portrayed with searing and total honesty, with all its painful intensity, as well as its contradictions. 'Save our daughter from me', the mother pleads with her husband, knowing that, despite her love, she can harm her daughter, scar her for life. Not many women have the courage to face this truth about themselves. How can we, when the idea of mothers being nothing but loving and nurturing infuses our thinking? Every other autorickshaw in Bangalore has the word Amma written on the back. The number of movies which have the word Amma in the title speak of what a popular and saleable idea it is. Motherhood as an abstraction, motherhood in the general, is sanctified. It is possible that the idea of the sanctity of the mother-child relationship comes from an awe for the act of creation. Look at the paintings and sculptures of mother and child, the songs and the poems about mother and child.

Yes, but what about individual mothers? Are all mother-child relationships beautiful, are all mothers as loving, protecting, and supporting as we want them to be, as we expect them to be? And what about unwed mothers? I think of Kunti in the Mahabharata and Hetty Sorrel in George Eliot's *Adam Bede*, two women, no, girls really, separated by time, space and cultures, frightened girls both of them, who try to get rid of their babies. Does the mother who is put on a pedestal then have, necessarily, to be a married woman?

Simone de Beauvoir gives us the ultimate single truth about motherhood. 'It is in maternity,' she says, 'that a woman fulfils her physiological destiny; her whole organic structure is adapted for the perpetuation of the species.' Hence the protective instinct, the nurturing instinct to help the child to survive. But we are not entirely children of Nature: we are evolved, social, civilised beings. We are thinking, feeling creatures, differing in this from all other animals. And, so too are there all kinds of mothers: loving mothers as well as unfeeling ones, kind mothers as well as cruel ones, protective mothers as well as possessive ones. The final truth is that we bring our selves into all our relationships. And therefore there is no such thing as The Mother; there is a woman who, at some point of time, becomes a mother. A mother is born when a woman gives birth to a child; nevertheless, the woman remains herself, her other qualities are still with her. She does not change, except for the qualities that this new relationship brings out in her, qualities which are confined to that relationship alone.

I read recently that Doris Lessing abandoned her children when she left South Africa and went to London. Does this make her a bad mother? I'm not so sure. Perhaps she recognised that she would not have been able to give the children what they needed, perhaps it was better for them to be with the father. I think of the question about why I mentioned my father and not my mother in my bio-data, and it seems to me that there's always a danger of down-sizing fatherhood, as there is of blowing up motherhood. There *are* a great many caring, loving fathers. Marilynne Robinson's two novels, *Gilead* and *Home*, have poignant portrayals of a deep and profound father's love. In Galsworthy's *Forsyte Saga*, when the children of Soames and Irene, old enemies, fall in love, it is Soames, Fleur's father, who comes off as the more unselfish parent. Willing to humble himself before Irene to give his daughter what she wants. Whereas, Irene, Jon's mother, despite telling her son, 'Do what you want, don't think of me,' is the one who finally breaks up the affair. Parenting is not, I would think, a place for gender politics.

And let's not forget that mothers can be, though rarely, cruel. Anandibai Joshi, India's first women doctor, was often punished by her mother with a burning stick plucked from the fire. There are other forms of cruelty too, which don't allow children to grow, which drain them of confidence in themselves. In contrast, there are adoptive mothers, and foster mothers, who can be as caring and protective as biological mothers. There are also mothers to whom motherhood is the one real experience of their lives and others who don't feel that way. I had a sister-in-law who said she felt lost unless she had a baby in the cradle; whereas, I felt a huge relief when my sons no longer needed me all day. There are also women who decide they will not have children. 'I am quite tired of so many children,' Jane Austen says in a letter to her sister Cassandra, speaking of a woman who was expecting her thirteenth child. And Virginia Woolf, while grieving over her childlessness, also confessed that she disliked the physicality of the process of giving birth.

Contradictions, ambiguities – no, motherhood is never simple. When my mother lay dying, I grieved, not for her dying, no, I prayed for a quick release. I grieved for the fact that we had so often been at loggerheads with each other, grieved that I had been unable to give her the unquestioning, unstinting love she demanded, which she thought was her right as a mother. And yet, after she died, each Sunday, which was the day when I had spent time with her, seemed blank. For months, I could do nothing during that time. And when the phone rang, at night or in the early morning, my heart still thudded in panic, thinking, 'It's Aai, something has happened to her.'

A complicated tangled relationship, indeed, born in blood and pain. Impossible to untangle. But there is no doubt that for most of us motherhood is a unique experience, one that goes deep within us, so deeply dyeing our beings that the colour never wholly fades. In a story about Kunti, I had Kunti think when she looks at her sons, long after the battle is over: *These old men my sons?* But that is how it is. Age makes no difference. Whatever their ages, mother and child remain mother and child.

Ultimately, when we cut out the cant, remove the frills, the assumptions, the stereotypes, the social and the religious constructs, what remains is a real and substantial relationship. To love and to be loved are the deepest desires of human beings. Only in this relationship of mother and child do we experience such a range of emotions, there is no other relationship as long-lasting, or as steadily strong, as this one. In fact, there nothing quite like it on this earth.

After a free and happy childhood and a conventional small-town education, SHASHI DESHPANDE slipped into marriage and motherhood, mainly because she didn't really know what she wanted to do. And then, baffled by finding herself where she was – mother of two sons and a full-time home-maker – she began to write, to understand why she was where she was and what it meant. Now, ten novels, four books for children, a number of collections of short stories, a book of non-fiction and a few translations later, she has realised that she is in a place she was meant to be, after all: in the midst of family, friends, books and writing. She has also discovered that the greatest joy of motherhood is that it leads to grandmotherhood!

Shashi Deshpande's novels include *That Long Silence, The Dark Holds no Terrors, A Matter of Time, Small Remedies* and *In the County of Deceit*. She was awarded the Padma Shri in 2008.

'Shake Her, She is Like the Tree that Grows Money!'

Contests and Critiques in Surrogacy

SAROJINI N. AND VRINDA MARWAH

This story is a narrativised version of an interview conducted by the authors with a surrogate in Delhi. Informed consent was taken, and a pre-decided and open-ended set of questions was used. The protagonist Meenu's[1] experiences reflect a constant and shifting negotiation with her realities, which reveals the agency she exerts even within a restrictive paradigm. Her body is her resource, and its use to earn money impacts her life in complex ways. In recent years, the sharp growth in commercial surrogacy in India has drawn much attention and raised several concerns. India's fertility industry is an integral part of the country's expanding medical tourism industry, within which commercial surrogacy is often portrayed as a beneficial and benevolent arrangement, which gives 'desperate and infertile' parents the child they want, and poor surrogate women the money they need. This complex and contemporary development not only splits motherhood in newer ways, it is able to push reproduction

[1] Names of persons, clinics and locations have been changed to protect the identities of persons involved.

from care to work, and from the private to the public, with implications for feminist praxis. Meenu's story amplifies the voices of surrogate women, and deepens our understanding of their contexts and choices. Her story is followed by an analysis of the surrogacy industry, as well as a critique of the proposed legislation to regulate this industry, both from a gender and public health perspective.

I left the hills of my childhood the first chance I got. I had been stuck with an unhappy life in my uncle's home after my parents died. I was quite young then. Without them, I found myself rudderless; nobody wanted to be responsible for me and everybody was discomfited by my presence. My uncle was especially unhappy to have me, perhaps understandably so, with a family of his own he could just about provide for. I made up my mind to leave as soon as I could. With no property, money or even family to call my own, there was nothing holding me back. And so I found Delhi. Or rather, Delhi found me. I got a job in a small private office. Although I didn't care for the work, and the salary wasn't much, I was glad to have a job.

It wasn't long before I married Sunil. Sunil, a lawyer, worked in the adjoining office to mine. We began by greeting each other, even stopping to chat briefly in the corridor. Soon we started going out for hours after work, often to stroll in public parks and sometimes, for a film. Our relationship grew, and over time Sunil was sure he wanted to marry me. But his parents were utterly unconvinced. I was Garhwali, and they wanted a Punjabi girl for their Punjabi boy. Although technically I was from a slightly higher caste than them, that went against me. They insisted that their *bahu* should be from the same caste as them. I didn't even have a family to speak of, and it followed that I would come with no money and no gifts. Sunil married me anyway, and they were furious.

Sunil's parents refused to talk to him at first, but he was their only son and soon enough they made up with him, without acknowledging me as part of their family. Even today I don't visit Sunil's parents' home; they are determined not to like me. They would complain to Sunil about my job, saying girls shouldn't be out of home so much. I quit my job to satisfy them, but nothing changed between us. They continued to ignore me. With time, even Sunil stopped trying to intervene. On his part, he made it a point to visit them at least once a fortnight. I was never welcome.

When Sunil and I couldn't conceive even after three years of marriage, that was all the prodding his parents needed. They started telling their son to leave me, since there was obviously something wrong with me. What kind of a woman can't even give her husband a child, they asked. They told him they would get him remarried, and this time to the 'right' girl. I was miserable, and Sunil was worried. So after some asking around, he found out about Dr Bhandari's Fertility Centre in Ghaziabad. Dr Bhandari's is an IVF clinic where many couples go for infertility treatment. It seemed a reliable and feasible option for us.

Dr Bhandari's Fertility Centre was housed in a residential colony in Ghaziabad, almost two hours away by bus from where we were. The reception area was small but packed, and the noticeboard had newspaper clippings of IVF babies delivered at the clinic. There were many pictures of twins, and even one of triplets. Sunil and I were both asked to undergo some preliminary tests. Sunil's test results were normal, but mine showed a blockage in my fallopian tubes. Dr Bhandari told us this could be cleared through medicines and a laproscopy, after which I would be able to conceive. He inquired about our finances. I told him I was without a job and Sunil had to get on without any help from his parents; it wasn't easy but we were managing somehow. The operation was a minor one, and in time, my son Sonu was born.

Some months later, Sunil had an accident. We had to spend nearly Rs 3,00,000 on his treatment. He had sustained many fractures, which would take a long time to heal. It was around this time that Dr Bhandari spoke to us about an offer. He suggested I be a surrogate mother for one of his clients, a Non-resident Indian (NRI) couple from London. We heard him out as he explained the procedure. He insisted it was good karma. Children are the life and soul of a home, and to help a woman be a mother is an act of God, he said. I would make enough money to clear all our debts *and* put some away.

The idea seemed bizarre at first. Though Dr Bhandari answered all of our questions, Sunil and I weren't convinced. But a few months on when Sunil was still recovering, we were badly stuck. Apart from daily expenses and rent, we had mounting debts. Our meager savings had run out in no time, and Dr Bhandari's offer sounded lucrative. We found ourselves reconsidering, and agreed that I should go ahead.

※

A child can have two mothers. Lord Krishna was born to Devaki but raised by Yashoda. A wife can have another man's child without sleeping with him. Kunti's sons were not her husband Pandu's, but were given his name and inheritance.

Dr Bhandari arranged everything. He insisted that I didn't need to meet the couple or bother with paperwork. Dr Bhandari assured me that I only had to take good care of myself and make sure I carry the pregnancy to term. They would use my egg and insert the man's semen into my uterus, he said. This confused me. If the egg was going to be mine, would I need to have intercourse with the man? That would be completely unacceptable, I began. Dr Bhandari clarified with much emphasis that this was not the case. The semen would be injected into my uterus. I wouldn't even meet the father.

Though I didn't sign anything, the terms of the arrangement were communicated verbally to me over and over again. No sex, no smoking and no drinking throughout the pregnancy. My husband should not accompany me to the clinic for check-ups or for the delivery. I would have no claim over the baby whatsoever. In case of a miscarriage, I would have to return whatever money I had received from the couple.

Since the NRI couple I was having the baby for was Sikh, they asked me to visit a gurudwara every week, so the foetus could imbibe his religion from the start. As a Hindu I did not really visit gurudwaras, but gradually I began to look forward to my gurudwara visits. It became my time away from everyone and everything else. The NRI couple even arranged for a domestic helper, Bimla, to look after my family and me. This was an unprecedented luxury for us. I'd never had someone else do my cooking and cleaning for me. I ate better food during my 'paid' pregnancy than I had during my own!

If Bimla was caring and careful with me, Sunil was the other extreme. He had been aloof to the surrogacy to begin with, but he grew resentful in no time. He would sulk and sneer at how careful I was being with this baby. Is it ours that you have to treat it like gold, he would say bitterly. Of course I had to be careful! We would have to return every paisa of the money we'd been spending with such abandon up till then. I was sure Sunil saw that too, but why he still chose to castigate me, I don't know.

Two weeks before my delivery date, I was admitted to the hospital. Though I didn't know it then, the NRI woman was also admitted at the same time. My labour was tough. I had problems till the last minute of the delivery. Finally they gave me an injection that made me unconscious. When I woke up, they told me a baby girl had been delivered. They had put five stitches on me.

The baby girl was very beautiful. She was handed over to her NRI parents the day she was born. The birth certificate was also prepared in their name. This was why the NRI woman had been brought to the hospital, so all the records would show her as having delivered the baby. I was relieved that they accepted the baby even though she was a girl. Their entire family was there to take her home.

Dr Bhandari had told me previously that it was best for me not to see her, and I had agreed then. But the nurse had said to me seconds after I regained consciousness, 'She is fair like you.' So I asked to see her. My chest was heavy when I handed her back to her NRI parents: I felt I was giving away my own child. But I knew it had to be done. She was theirs. They would give her a good life.

❈❈

I returned home after two days of rest at the hospital, from the birth of a daughter I would never know. Sunil had told our friends and neighbours that our baby died from complications during labour. They gathered around me briefly, sympathizing, advising me to reconcile with the death as God's will. It made me uncomfortable to hear them talk like that about a baby whose long and happy life I was praying for inside. So much felt unsettled then; Sonu would seek Bimla for days, but she was gone.

Sunil is a different person now. I had recognised from the beginning that I would have to take care of this pregnancy by myself, but I hadn't anticipated the extent of Sunil's hostility. After all, the decision to go in for surrogacy had been ours together. We had agreed it was the best way out of our troubles, but he just could not accept the arrangement. Just the other day, our son got after Sunil to buy him a toy helicopter. I could see that Sunil was beginning to get annoyed. Suddenly he snapped, 'Why don't you ask your lovely mother? She can buy it for you. Shake her, she is like the tree that grows money!' I was stunned. I couldn't believe he would humiliate me with such a comparison.

But his feelings were clear. He may have wanted the money, but he could not accept the pregnancy.

He avoids taking me anywhere now, and has started visiting his parents every other day. They are probably telling him to leave me. Our marriage is hanging by a thread, and that thread is our son. Can I leave Sunil? Will people let a woman live without her husband and with her child? I don't know, but I have little faith.

I have decided to be a surrogate again. Of course, I will have to move to a new neighborhood. My friends and relatives might wonder, but that can be sorted out. I want to earn more money. Sunil won't stop me; I know he wants the money too. With a large sum, we can buy our own place and save for my son's studies. But this will have to be the last time.

I now communicate with Dr Bhandari on a regular basis. Dr Bhandari has helped me, but he has also exploited me. I found out from the nursing home that while he gave me only 2 lakhs for the surrogacy, he was given 15 lakhs by the couple from London. I have satisfied myself with the thought that he helped us out in a crisis, but I will not be cheated like this again. I will ask for 5 lakhs this time. I will not bring my price down, and I will insist on the paperwork.

I am also something of a surrogacy agent for Dr Bhandari now. Since Dr Bhandari keeps really busy, he asked me if I wanted to manage his surrogacy advertisements for him. So I advertise for surrogates in local newspapers and women's magazines. The doctors here know me quite well. They call when they need surrogates from good families. Young women call looking to be surrogates. They are usually in low-income and low-status jobs, and can be easily exploited by doctors, agents and clients alike. I try to get them a fair deal. I do what I can, but we need legal contracts. We should get more money. We need guarantees.

❊❊

We can provide you an Indian surrogate recruited through advertisements in our local newspapers. All surrogates taken into our program are between 21–35 years of age. They are married with previous normal deliveries and healthy babies.[2]

We select only few of the many surrogate mom(s) that we screen, who are in the best of health, having good reproductive history, free of any sexually transmitted diseases, and importantly who have the fervour to support someone to make their family complete.[3]

The above advertisements appear on websites offering infertility treatment and surrogacy services. In recent years, the practice of commercial surrogacy in India has grown significantly, and achieved the proportions of an industry. Surrogacy is the practice of gestating a child for another couple or individual, and involves the use of Assisted Reproductive Technologies (ARTs), such as In Vitro Fertilisation (IVF) or test tube baby technology, and Intra Uterine Insemination (IUI) or artificial insemination, as well as additional combinations such as Intra Cytoplasmic

[2] Accessed on 1st April 2010 from: http://wewantababy.com/index.php?option=com_content&view=article&id=26&Itemid=95

[3] Accessed on 1st April 2010 from: http://surrogacyindia.com/ip_Selectingsurrogate.html

Sperm Injection (ICSI), used for male factor infertility, etc. Surrogacy is a growing part of India's medical tourism industry, which has earned the country tags such as 'global doctor' and 'mother destination'. Indeed, it is the 'First World skill' that India offers at 'Third World prices', along with benefits such as English-speaking doctors, easy availability of women willing to be surrogates and egg donors, and world-famous tourist spots, that make it so attractive for baby-seekers. A considerable boost to the industry is provided by the context and nature of its operation – lack of regulation makes the fertility industry in particular, and the private medical market more generally, attractive to users, with short waits, few forms and next to no red tape. In addition, the Indian government aids the promotion of medical tourism by allowing private hospitals treating overseas patients to enjoy lower import duties on medical supplies and lower tax rates.

While official statistics on the number of surrogacies being arranged in India are not available, anecdotal evidence suggests a sharp increase. Anand (Gujarat), once the milk capital of the country, is now better known as the surrogate mother hub of the world as infertile couples from various countries come in search of wombs for hire, often with specifications such as skin colour, religion and educational background. In mainstream accounts, commercial surrogacy is often portrayed as a beneficial and benevolent arrangement, which gives 'desperate and infertile' parents the child they want, and poor surrogate women the money they need. However, a more considered understanding of surrogacy reveals that ethical, economic and political questions are contained in issues commonly regarded as personal.

Reproduction, and its more recent avatar of technologically-assisted reproduction, is a site of inquiry that feminists have dislodged from the domain of the strictly biological, medical, private and the familial. In surrogacy, the commodification of the body is clear; the child becomes a product of the arrangement while the woman's body becomes a 'resource'. Some (Ketchum 1989) consider surrogacy arrangements illegitimate and unethical, and equate these to women selling their bodies and babies. This view considers reproduction special, and considers its commercialisation degrading. Others (Nussbaum 1998, Shah 2009) emphasise the need to critically assess the reasons for why certain occupations related to women's sexual and reproductive capacity are stigmatised. Notions of chastity and naturalness have been used to control and domesticate all such labour, and through it, women. For instance, it is the very 'special' mother-child relationship that enables men to avoid equal childrearing responsibilities, and maintains gender inequality in income patterns, which in turn ensures that women remain economically dependent, especially when they have children (Morgan 1985). Perhaps we should consider that women's reproduction has always been – and continues to be – a political exchange, in that it occurs through unequal power relations, is subject to control, and is done in the service of diverse ends, including material, social, emotional, and familial privilege. Why, then, are women who are commercial surrogates seen as doing something new and different, complex and controversial?

Are we guilty, as Pande (2010) suggests, of being moralistic only when the bodies of poor women are in focus?

At the same time, commercial surrogacy is a complex development that is able to not only push reproduction from the private sphere of family to the public space of the market – from care to work – but is also able to split motherhood in new ways. Commercial surrogacy could potentially create three mothers – the social or commissioning mother, the genetic mother (egg donor), and the gestational mother (surrogate) – with potentially conflicting claims over the child. In case of a legal contest, does a commissioning mother's 'procreative intent' trump a surrogate's biological link and gestational labour? That will depend on how we are defining motherhood, and in particular, biology. Here it is important to remember that the body and its biology is made, and made meaningful, only within socio-cultural, economic and political processes. Commercial surrogacy is making up and making real biology as it goes along. Menon (2011) quotes Emily Martin to point out that science is an 'interpretive exercise'. While surrogacy may create three mothers – the gestational, the genetic and the social – which mother the child belongs to, however, is discursively constituted, and stamped with biology, depending on the case at hand. In commercial gestational surrogacy, the commissioning couple is told the child is theirs since the gametes and genes are theirs. In contrast, a woman who is gestating the baby she intends to raise, but has used donor egg, is told by the same medical establishment that the baby is hers because the blood is hers, and the cells from which the baby is growing are hers.

Here, as Menon argues, science is engaged in constituting the natural, rather than only objectively identifying it. Thus, biology itself becomes contested, and a site where other contesting claims play out.

Feminist critiques of surrogacy have highlighted that the ART industry lies at the intersection of patriarchy and market, wherein these technologies meet rather than question the pressure on women to be mothers. These are expensive technologies with low success rates and significant health risks, and their 'demand' comes from and reinforces a culture that glorifies motherhood and biological determinism over other options such as adoption or even voluntary childlessness. Yet, these technologies are also delinking biology – indeed sex – from reproduction by making it possible for gay individuals and couples, and single persons, to have biologically related children. When a single woman or a gay couple chooses ARTs or surrogacy, are they honouring the biological in kinship relations and thus conforming to heteronormative institutions? Or are they disrupting the holy trinity of the father-mother-child, and in doing so, subverting in some fundamental ways, gender socialisation, gender role associations, the division of labour and notions of a correct parenthood. Or is it a bit of both?

While it cannot be said that alternative family formations are by definition non-oppressive or non-patriarchal, it can be said that such families challenge the typical formats through which patriarchy has conducted itself. Gay and single persons have long been considered and treated as outsiders to family and marriage, and all the privileges that these inter-linked institutions confer.

Perhaps the most significant piece of the surrogacy puzzle is the political economy context of women's labour under globalisation. As Sunder Rajan suggests, emergent biotechnologies such as ARTs can be understood only by 'simultaneously analyzing the market frameworks within which they emerge' (2006: 33). With privatisation and liberalisation, recent decades have seen a rise in informalisation and sexualisation of women's work; indigenous livelihoods are being destroyed and the state is rolling back from social spending, leaving poor women with few work options. In the Indian subcontinent today, women who are garment workers, sex workers, and surrogates, are engaged in contemporary and commercial forms of sexual/ised and reproductive labour – all of which were generally, traditionally considered economically non-productive, apart from being seen as dignified only if domesticated. These jobs are characterised by low wages, long hours, insecurity of tenure, as well as inattention to health and rights. One has to ask then, is it free 'choice' that leads women to be surrogates, or a lack of 'real choice'? It is this question that has led some feminists to go beyond a framework of reproductive rights of surrogates, and to ask also for reproductive justice. Reproductive justice advocates (Lingam 1998, Bailey 2011) question the market-conferred right of poor women to sell their reproductive labour, without affording them the justice of a living wage, quality education, affordable health care, freedom from violence, and real reproductive autonomy. Meenu represents a class of women in India who have little say about when and how they reproduce, and are often victims of coercive population control measures, high maternal morbidity and mortality, STIs, and so on.

It is this other side, the seamy underbelly of this well-advertised, supposedly 'win-win' industry, that needs our attention. Globalisation creates the disturbing phenomenon of a race-to-the-bottom; as has been seen with the textile and electronics industries, competition may force surrogates to settle for lower and lower fees. There is enough anecdotal evidence to suggest that surrogates and donors are chosen on the basis of their caste, religion, skin colour, attractiveness, etc. In the marriage of free market and neo-eugenics, does anything go? Studies (Saravanan 2010, Pande 2010) have also pointed out that surrogates have limited autonomy over their contract pregnancies. Surrogates are often chosen based on their submissiveness to the demands of doctors and intended parents. Through processes such as recruitment, contract and counselling, the perfect surrogate – cheap, docile, selfless and nurturing – is created. These women are often poor and poorly educated, and once selected, have to submit to several rules – some clinics make it mandatory for women to stay at surrogate homes, while others provide them with separate family accommodation away from their permanent residences. They have little or no say in decisions, including decisions about their own bodies. For instance, they have no right to choose the terms of relinquishment of the baby; the clinics decide whether the baby is handed over to the intended parents immediately or soon after birth.

Clearly, commercial surrogacy becomes an explosive site in the encounter between gender, technology and society, one that is blurring the boundaries of women's bodies, and of the body of feminist praxis. Stories like that of Meenu's highlight some of what can go wrong when surrogacy is practised in a legal vacuum. It is such stories that should in turn inform feminist politics when we advocate for greater protections and rights for these women, who are probably the most vulnerable part of the fertility industry.

※※

The proposed legislation to regulate the fertility industry, the Draft Assisted Reproductive Technology (Regulation) Bill and Rules 2010[4], has been prepared by the Indian Council of Medical Research (ICMR), in a welcome step. Since this is in draft form, a gender and rights perspective can be employed to critique some provisions of this Bill and make it more inclusive.

- According to the present draft Bill, payment to the surrogate is to be made in five installments, with the majority, i.e. 75 per cent of the payment, to be made as the fifth and final installment, following the delivery of the child. This is highly imbalanced and unfavourable to the surrogate, and a more equitable distribution of payment in the form of equal installments is desirable.
- Many serious health risks (procedural and drug-related, for both the woman and the child) need to be acknowledged and mentioned in the consent form. The

[4] Ministry of Health and Family Welfare and Indian Council of Medical Research (2010): *Draft Assisted Reproductive Technologies (Regulation) Bill and Rules – 2010.*

consent form should also mention, where relevant, that the long term effects of drugs and procedures in ARTs are under-researched.

- The Bill mentions that the commissioning parent(s) shall ensure that the surrogate mother and the child she delivers are 'appropriately' insured; while this is indeed necessary, more elaboration is required on the nature and extent of insurance that will be provided, particularly with regard to post-delivery follow-up and care, failing which the commissioning parent(s) and the overseeing clinic should be held legally responsible.

- The draft states that ARTs will be available to all single persons, married couples and unmarried couples. However, couple is defined as two persons 'having a sexual relationship that is legal in India'. In addition, the bill defines both married and unmarried couples, as being in a marriage or relationship respectively that is legal in the country of which they are citizens. As such, it is not clear how these three definitions will be read together, and if ARTs will be available for gay couples, particularly Indian gay couples. This needs to be clarified and ascertained from a rights perspective, without any discrimination, since homosexuality has been decriminalised (but not legalised) in India.

- According to the Bill, only gestational surrogacy, i.e. through In Vitro Fertilisation (IVF) and Embryo Transfer (ET), will be permitted, and genetic surrogacy, i.e. through Intra Uterine Insemination (IUI) will not. By ruling out genetic surrogacy, the bill seeks to foreclose the possibility of any contesting claims over the baby by the surrogate mother, thus preserving the contract. Yet, genetic surrogacy through IUI where possible remains a less commercial and less invasive option, and avoids the excessive use of IVF for obtaining donor eggs. Thus, genetic surrogacy should be an option.

- The 2010 draft permits multiple embryo implantation (up to three), which increases the chances of achieving pregnancy, but also carries additional health risks. Further, in case of 'exceptional circumstances' such as elderly women, poor embryo quality etc., this upper limit does not hold. This raises concerns about exposing women already more vulnerable due to their age etc., to even greater health risks. The world over, there is a move towards single embryo implantation in view of health risks to mother and child due to foetal reduction and multiple pregnancy. Thus, in India too, single embryo implantation, including under 'exceptional circumstances', should be considered.

- Independent and long term counselling should be available for the surrogate.

- In view of her vulnerable position, the provision of a state-sponsored legal counsel for the surrogate should be mandatory in all surrogacy arrangements, to oversee the contract, its preservation and any legal contests on behalf of the surrogate.

- The bill mandates the appointment of a local guardian in case of surrogacy arrangements where the intended couple is staying outside India. This local guardian will be legally obliged to take delivery of the child born of the surrogacy arrangement if the intended couple does not do so. It appears that the local guardian may hand over such a child to an adoption agency, or bring him/her up. This is a significant responsibility, and as such, the role of the local guardian needs to be clearly demarcated and overseen to prevent abuse.

- In lieu of the recent and controversial cases of international surrogacy that have resulted in legal battles for citizenship status for the child/ren, the 2010 Draft Bill has made provisions to address this issue. Now, the draft ART Bill 2010 mandates that any foreign couple accessing surrogacy in India must produce a certificate from their country declaring that it permits surrogacy, and will recognise the child/ren born out of surrogacy as its legal citizen/s.

Therefore, it can be concluded that while a legislation to regulate the untrammeled commercialisation of ARTs and surrogacy in India is a much-needed step towards checking unethical medical practice, the rights of surrogates – legal, financial, and medical – still need to be better protected. The ART industry has flourished because of global trade systems and the business of making mothers and babies. However, the human rights component of issues emerging in the contemporary encounter of globalisation, technology, labour and gender requires greater attention.

References

Bailey, A. (2011) Reconceiving Surrogacy: Toward a Reproductive Justice Account of Indian Surrogacy. *Hypatia*, 715–741.

Ketchum, S.A. (1989) Seeling Babies and Selling Bodies. *Hypatia,* 116–127.

Lingam, *Lakshmi* (1998) (ed) Reproductive Technologies and Violation of Women's Bodies. In: *Understanding Women's Health Issues: A Reader.* New Delhi: Kali for Women.

Menon, N. (2011) The disappearing body and feminist thought. Retrieved September 17, 2011, from www.kafila.org: http://kafila.org/2011/02/18/the-disappearing-body-and-feminist-thought/

Morgan, Derek. (1985) Making Motherhood Male: Surrogacy and the Moral Economy of Women. *Journal of Law and Society.* 12 (2): 219–238.

Nussbaum, M. (1998) Whether from Reason or Prejudice: Taking Money for Bodily Services. *The Journal of Legal Studies,* 693–723.

Palattiyil, G., E. Blyth, D. Sidhva, and G. Balakrishnan (2010) Globalization and cross-border reproductive services: Ethical implications of surrogacy in India for social work. *International Social Work,* 53 (5): 686–700.

Pande, A. (2009) Not an 'Angel', Not a 'Whore': Surrogates as 'Dirty' Workers in India. *Indian Journal of Gender Studies,* 16(2): 141–173.

Pande, A (2010) Commercial Surrogacy in India: Manufacturing a Perfect Mother-worker. *Journal of Women in Culture and Society,* 35(4): 969–992.

Rajan, K.S. (2006) *Biocapital: The Constitution of Post-genomic Life.* Durham: Duke University Press.

Sama Resource Group for Women and Health (2010): *Constructing Conceptions: The Mapping of Assisted Reproductive Technologies in India.* New Delhi.

Saravanan, S. (2010) Transnational Surrogacy and Objectification of Gestational Mothers. *Economic and Political Weekly,* 26–29.

Shah, C. (2009) Surrogate Motherhood and Women's Sexual and Reproductive Rights. Paper presented at the Consultation, My body, my life, my rights: Addressing violations of women's sexual and reproductive rights, Asia Pacific Forum on Women, Law and Development: Thailand.

Smerdon, U. R. (2008) Crossing Bodies, Crossing Borders: International Surrogacy between the United States and India. *Cumberland Law Review*, 39 (1): 15–85.

SAROJINI NADIMPALLY is with Sama-Resource Group for Women and Health, a Delhi-based women's organisation, and has been a women's health activist for the last twenty years. She has been actively campaigning against the two-child norm, population control policies, sex-selective abortions, hazardous contraceptive technologies, unethical conduct of clinical trials on marginalised communities, and issues related to human rights and violence (including communal). She has been involved in research and advocacy around issues related to assisted reproductive technologies including surrogacy, and maternal health and health systems. Sarojini was the Convenor of the Medico Friends Circle (MFC) and co-coordinated the MFC fact finding committee that studied the impact of health after the Gujarat riots of 2002 and contributed largely to the report, 'Carnage in Gujarat: A Public Health Crisis'. She is also the Joint Convenor of Jan Swasthya Abhiyan, the Indian chapter of the People's Health Movement. Recently she has been a part of the fact finding on Maternal Deaths and Denial of Maternal Care in Barwani District, Madhya Pradesh: Issues and Concerns and the unethical implementation of HPV vaccine 'demonstration projects' in the tribal areas of Andhra Pradesh. She has contributed several articles to national as well as international journals and co-authored a book, *Touch Me, Touch Me Not: Women, Plants and Healing* published by Kali for Women, Delhi.

VRINDA MARWAH is based in Delhi, and works on gender and sexuality from a feminist perspective. She was Program Coordinator at Sama

Resource Group for Women and Health, where she worked on gender, health and technologies at research, capacity building, and policy advocacy levels. She has written extensively on assisted reproductive technologies and commercial surrogacy, and on questions of sexual identity and terminologies. Vrinda is now with Creating Resources for Empowerment in Action (CREA), a feminist human rights organisation. Vrinda completed her undergraduate studies from the University of Delhi and her post-graduate studies from the University of London. Her work on commercial surrogacy has made her especially interested in the politics of reproduction, and the kinds of questions it makes possible and impossible to ask.

The authors would like to thank Meenu, and all team members of Sama. The arguments and conclusions in the essay are the personal opinions of the authors.

The Gardener's Daughter

SARITA MANDANNA

I know what I will be in my next life. No, I am not yet dead. My body clings to life with all the strength left in these bones, and God knows I can fight. But it draws closer, the end. I feel it, in the shift of the wind. I lie here with little more to fill my days than stare endlessly at the front garden and the fountains and, in this skeletal tick of the hours, I have worked it out.

Coming back as a bird would be too easy. Twittering foolishly from the trees, spending the mornings dipping and wheeling in the breeze. Death when it came might be vicious – a well aimed catapult or pellet, or the swift gouge of a cat's claws perhaps. A paltry price all the same for a life of careless liberty. Our dogs lead better lives than we do, cuddled and cosseted, romping unfettered about our homes. An earthworm? What purpose would that serve, to scuttle blindly in the mud with neither awareness nor aspiration?

No. It is my karma to come back as one of the helps. Blank-faced, with shiny, dark skin and kinks in my hair, the stink of sweat trapped in my armpits. And what if He decides to leave me with some vestige of memory? So that I know in my heart that this is not right, neither this hovel nor the man rutting above me, flashes of memory just out of my reach, of silk and gold and carved rosewood? Wouldn't that be the ultimate irony, Garima Thakore back at Basera, unrecognisable even to herself?

***

The Mustang paused, contemplating its final climb. The iron gates lay directly ahead, flung wide open to allow us passage, draped with garlands of mango leaves and marigolds, massive torches jammed into the earth on either side. 'BAS' on the gate to my left, in elaborate scrollwork, 'ERA' on the other, glowing red in the flickering light and casting dancing shadows on the ground. The house loomed ahead, gigantic and ablaze with light, like the wedding cake we'd cut some hours before. My pulse quickened at the knot of people gathered on the verandah, and I shifted slightly in my seat. So this is where I would spend the rest of my life, at the side of this man staring outside the car window. He'd spoken not one word the entire way from the reception.

My brother Raja, entrusted with chaperoning us to Basera had tried to make conversation, twisting cheerfully around from the front seat to grumble over how expensive liquor was getting, enquire about the horsepower on the Mustang and gossip about the new Commissioner of Police. Growing discouraged with the monosyllabic replies he'd received however, even he'd lapsed into silence a half an hour ago.

I understood though. It was late and my husband – my *husband!* – must be exhausted. It'd been a long day of fire and rituals and repeating of chants, capped by an elaborate reception where everything in the hotel ballroom – the crystal, the chandeliers, even the guests, had appeared to my dazzled eyes to shimmer. When it was time for us, the bride and bridegroom, to leave, Papa had been stiff-faced, trying to conceal his tears as he said his goodbyes. Much as I loved my father, all I felt on the other hand, was elation.

What was there to be sad about? Such an honour, this proposal, from one of the oldest families in the city. Yes, I was blessed with my mother's skin, and had my grandmother's eyes. Our family was a respected one besides, advisors for generations to the Nizams of old; one of my uncles had been a recognised poet. Still, we were certainly not wealthy, not any more, not by any standards. When I turned nineteen and my parents started to look for a boy, I thought I might marry a doctor, or someone with a good job in Madras or Bangalore. Never did we expect a proposal for Jayanta Thakore's only son, Vijayant. My father said the only thing he could: 'Yes.'

Pleased as she had been, Ma had also been apprehensive. 'He's a big man, Thakore Sahib,' she fretted, 'they have moneyed ways.' She twisted the ends of her pallu, worried. 'Watch them, learn their habits,' she advised. 'Keep your mouth shut. Fit in with the family.'

I stepped from the car now, careful not to trip over my sari. My mother-in-law stood at the entrance, delicate and regal in Japanese silk, diamonds sparkling around her neck. I bent to touch her feet. An American lady, a family friend I recognised from the reception, stood to her side. Suddenly unsure of what to do, I foolishly reached for her feet as well.

'Oh no, no!' my mother-in-law exclaimed laughing. 'There's no need for that. You met Diane earlier this evening. Just say hello. I'm sorry,' she continued, turning to the woman, 'all these customs…'

V exhaled impatiently behind me. He strode up to them, kissed their cheeks and walked on inside. Not turning once for his brand new bride.

❦

Looking back now, I see that my life has been clearly divided into two parts – before I was married, and after. Some years ago, when I met Megha, my cousin from Ma's side after a gap of nearly thirty years, it had felt to me as if time had melted away. Seeing her took me right back to when we had been the best of friends, eating golgappas by the dozen and sneaking away from school to watch the latest Dharmendra movie.

We were sitting holding hands and reminiscing when – 'You've changed,' she suddenly exclaimed. 'Where is the laughing girl I remember so well? You have become so… impressive. Like a school principal.'

At the time, it had come pat to my tongue – 'That was a long time ago Megha, before we were married. How can I be seen giggling with all this grey hair now?'

She shook her head wryly. 'You've grown into your name,' she commented.

It was only later that I wondered which version of my name she had meant. Garima, the dignified, or Garima, the proud?

❀

Don't misunderstand me: much of the change I welcomed. I was determined to be the best daughter-in-law this family had ever seen. 'Call us Mummy and Daddy,' Mummy suggested lightly, and I began at once. I watched the way she walked, her head thrown back, brooch pinned to her sari, perfectly straight and exactly two inches beneath her shoulder. She never crossed her knees, I noticed, only her ankles. I even studied her feet, the way she pointed them downwards when she sat. I learned to cut apples into wafer thin circles instead of the fat chunks that I was used to, to eat fish cutlets and Russian salad with forks and knives, no more satisfying licking my fingers clean of the last drip of curry. I watched, and I learned.

This was a reserved family, quite different from my sisters and our parents, Ma admonishing Papa to 'control his wind' even as he insisted it was only a motorcycle going past, *putt putt putt*. I grew up with raised voices and laughter, with the hustle and bustle of family and neighbours through our lived-in home. At Basera, however, everything was hushed and well mannered. We dressed for dinner and said 'Please' and 'Thank you' to one another in modulated, perfectly pronounced syllables.

Mummy glided about the garden, not really given to heart-to-heart talks with her daughter-in-law, or indeed anyone at all. V and she were close though. Mother and son had but to look at each other, just a flicker of an expression or the twitch of an identical, hooked eyebrow and each would immediately know what the other was thinking.

They laughed at the same jokes and read the same books, so effortlessly in tune that they almost seemed to finish the other's sentences. Large, bluff Daddy was the odd one out. He shared an uneasy truce with his son. When V's sarcasm hit a nerve and Daddy would snap back, it was Mummy who'd step in, placing a cool hand upon his arm. She'd throw a warning look at V who'd subside at once, turning back to his plate with a small, satisfied smile. It made me envious, their connection. I couldn't wait to forge one like that for myself.

In the meantime, there were dinner invitations and countless evenings at the Club. We had supper parties every other Saturday, elaborate affairs when the rosewood eighteen-seater would be laid with the family porcelain. Thomas, the Keralite butler would serve us pomfret béarnaise, and chicken with forty cloves of garlic, as the room filled with the clink of silver and the latest political and business chatter from Delhi and Bombay.

I listened intently to these conversations. Papa had insisted that all of his daughters be educated, in spite of Ma's protests that too much studying could make a girl headstrong, and which man would ever want a wife like that? Papa laughed and brushed her concerns aside, having us read the newspapers every single morning, front page to the last.

When, not long after V and I were married, the government arbitrarily declared a state of Emergency in the country, no-one was more disheartened than Papa. He recalled the idealism of the freedom struggle. Was this what his generation had fought for? It was *adharm*, he said, the highest travesty of justice. I agreed. My cousins talked angrily of protest marches and hunger strikes, exclaiming with disgust over the photographs of arrested politicians each day in the newspapers, so many, taken away in shackles.

Little, however, changed at Basera. We hosted our Saturday dinners and entertained our connections, talking sideways and around the Emergency as if it was all happening elsewhere. I watched, and I followed, but in my heart, I was doubtful. Shouldn't the Thakores, one of the most prominent families of the city, be doing something more?

I held my tongue as long as I could. In the end however, it got away with me, exactly as Ma constantly worried it would.

It was a beautiful summer evening, and we'd served dinner in the garden for a change. Thomas had just brought out the main course; I even remember that it was quail. Maybe it was the wine I had drunk, a little over my self-imposed, one-glass limit. Perhaps it was the attar that had been dabbed on the garden lights to mask the smell of the mosquito coils. A heady scent of *raat ki rani*, wafting over the table and making me nostalgic for the plant that Papa tended with such care in his garden.

The conversation was the usual roundabout discussion of the Emergency, the jokes about getting things to work and having to grease enough palms. Mishraji, a family friend, he of the long political reach and the fat, stubby fingers that were always feeling up whichever woman was closest, made a wisecrack about All *Indira* Radio, and everyone burst out laughing. I looked at V, sprawled in his chair, a sardonic, slightly bored expression on his face as he twirled the ice in his glass and stared into the night. I opened my mouth and began to talk. I looked straight at him, only him, as I talked of *dharm*, of duty, of the founding fathers of the country, of the shame they would have felt at the state of the country, at the lot of us sitting here in our enameled chairs and doing little more than cracking gentle jokes.

The table fell silent. I began to flush as too late, I realised all I'd said. 'I believe our daughter-in-law here,' Daddy said, his voice cutting right through me, 'may have had a little too much wine.'

I tumbled from my self-righteous perch in a hurry, gulping out an apology and excusing myself from dinner. I fled to our bedroom, my cheeks burning, and wept for hours into the pillow, uncaring of the eyeliner that seeped into the silk. I finally fell asleep, exhausted from waiting for V.

Mummy came to our bedroom the next morning. 'That was quite a performance,' she said, 'and totally unnecessary.' I stared puffy eyed at the floor. She sighed. 'Your world, Garima,' she said, 'is this house and this family. There's far more that can be achieved by compromise and diplomacy than in drawing a line in the sand. Politicians come and go. Emergency or not, whether this government or another, all that matters is that this family thrives.'

I thought of my father, how gallant he must have looked in his Gandhi topi, of the way his eyes shone behind his glasses when he talked of righteousness and liberty. 'Yes, Mummy,' I said.

❈

It was Mummy's idea for V to take me to Paris. We'd not yet had a proper honeymoon, she pointed out, and besides, it would give Daddy time to get over his anger. It was wonderful. It was the first time I had flown anywhere, let alone visited Europe. The unrest back home seemed far removed as we strolled down the Champs-Élysées, and posed for pictures at the Eiffel Tower. I even cajoled V into taking a cruise down the Seine one evening.

As V lay in my arms one night, I asked if Daddy shouldn't do more against the Emergency.

He was silent awhile. Just when I thought he'd fallen asleep, he said, 'At Basera, we tow the middle road. There is no right or wrong: only protocol.'

I traced the grey in his hairline and thought back to the letters I'd found in our bedroom bureau. Letters folded and refolded so many times, they were cracking along the folds. Letters addressed to 'My very own,' and ending with 'Forever, Diane.' There'd been a photograph among them, of a laughing V, laughing the way he sometimes did with the dogs and never with me, his arms around a tall, sweet-faced girl, both of them in Stanford T-shirts in matching midnight blue.

❈

Soon after we returned, I found I was pregnant. There is significant power in bringing forth the next generation. I'd already taken over the running of the kitchen, and now the help came to me for everything – selecting new curtains, managing the household accounts, drawing up guest lists. I grew more confident, slowly adding touches of my own to the house. I had the second pantry converted into a pooja room, moving the Gods from their dingy alcove and showering them with jasmine and roses each morning. The brass lamps were hauled out from the attic and I interlaced their chain links with paddy from the fields that the family owned, deep in the interiors of the state. I taught the cook to make pulao like Ma did, and to serve poha at the breakfast table, alongside the toast and Seville marmalade.

Daddy was thrilled – 'Just like my mother used to make,' he said of the pulao. Mummy smiled vaguely too, although I hardly think she noticed what went into that slender frame of hers. And V… I believe he appreciated all I did too. He never said anything outright, but then he never objected either when I plied his plate with more.

All the while, I thought of the child growing inside me. It was a boy, I was certain of it. I already had a name picked out: Adarsh. The principled one.

'Think good thoughts,' Ma instructed, 'it makes for a happy baby.' I thought all kinds of thoughts, talking all day in my head with my son, reading aloud to him from the Gita and the Ramayan, and all forty verses of the Hanuman Chalisa.

It was an omen, I knew, when Adarsh kicked in my womb for the first time that November, just as we were listening to Mrs Gandhi's broadcast: 'We felt that the country has developed a disease and, if it is to be cured soon, it has to be given a dose of medicine, even if it is a bitter dose. However dear a child may be, if the doctor has prescribed bitter pills for him, they have to be administered for his cure.'

I listened, aghast. To equate this mockery of justice with *motherhood*! 'The child may sometimes cry,' she continued, 'and we may have to say, "Take the medicine, otherwise you will not get cured".' It was at that exact moment that Adarsh kicked, as if in protest, so hard that I cried out in astonishment.

'Now when a child suffers, the mother suffers too.'

Adarsh kicked again, vigorously. I cradled my stomach in my arms, shutting my eyes in gratitude for this child, for this very special child.

⁂

I grew ever more adroit at managing our guests, knowing when to keep my mouth shut and just when to crack the right sort of jokes. We had the CEO of an American conglomerate visiting one evening, along with Mishraji and a high-ranking bureaucrat from the ministry. Nobody talked outright about the transaction at hand – that would be crass – although from the frustrated tone of the American as he talked about the rampant red tapeism, and the increasing bluster of the bureaucrat, it was obvious that things were not going well. Touching a fork to a glass, I smiled and claimed feminine privilege in hijacking the conversation.

Had they, I asked, heard the one about the newly minted Indian minister who travels to America? He's amazed by the lifestyle of his host, a senator, and asks him how he can possibly afford this beautiful mansion and manicured grounds on his modest salary.

The senator points out the window. 'Do you see the river out there?' The minister nods. 'The bridge over the river?' The minister nods again. The senator winks. 'Ten per cent.'

A year later, the senator visits the minister in India and is astounded by the staggering opulence of the latter's home. The minister points him to the window. 'You see the river?' The senator nods. 'The bridge over the river?' 'No,' the senator says, puzzled, 'I don't see any bridge.' The minister winks. 'A hundred per cent.'

The men stared incredulously at me for a second and then burst out laughing, all of them. The joke wasn't even my own. Under the table, I touched my hand to my belly, willing my son to listen, and learn.

❈

I went home for my confinement, but it felt cramped, our little house. My head ached from the constant company. I carted my oversized stomach from room to room, listless and pining for V. Ma sensed this. 'You're missing them, aren't you? It's as it should be,' she said, waving aside my protests. I went back to Basera soon after.

I went ten days over my due date, our women friends sympathising with what they thought must be my impatience to get this pregnancy over with. Quite the contrary. I treasured each extra day. Adarsh held safe inside the cocoon of my body, just him and me for a few days more. I talked and sang and hummed to him, and he'd kick against my belly to let me know he was listening. Sometimes it was a tiny fist, imprinted against my skin. I'd reach my fingers to it, and it would rest there for a second against my hand, before withdrawing once more into my womb.

When he finally arrived, on the heels of a long and protracted delivery, it was the first thing I did, to touch my fingers to his bunched up fist. 'Adarsh,' I said his name out aloud, and he turned at the sound of my voice. I held my son in his arms for the first time, and felt a jolt of emotion so strong that I could barely speak. I would gladly die, I knew, than let a hair on this fragile, tiny head come to harm.

✦

We had more children. Kishen, Shanti and pretty Leela. Adarsh, however, he was my – our – first. Special. I'd feed him, and I swear to you, would feel in my own stomach a bloated fullness when the boy was done. I'd get up in the middle of the night, knowing instinctively that he needed me although he'd still be asleep in his crib. He'd awaken just as I'd approach the door of the nursery, crying out from colic, or a budding tooth. The night nurse would still be rubbing the sleep from her eyes and I would already have him on my lap. The connection I had so wanted, it was real. Adarsh and I were conjoined, as if by an invisible umbilical cord.

Still, as these things go, it was not me who Adarsh loved the most. It was his father. I was his dal roti, his comfort blanket, the balm on his wounds. It was V, however, who took top billing with our son, effortlessly, without trying to, or indeed even noticing just how much the child adored him.

I didn't mind. How could I, when I loved them both so?

✦

We had more children. Basera was filled with the sound of baby voices and running feet. Each one so different. Tall, thin Kishen with the look of Mummy about him. A quiet, sensitive, intelligent child, his nose perpetually buried in a book. Shanti, the clown of the family, forever dancing and singing. Leela, instinctively sweet-natured, and her grandfather's pet.

And Adarsh... big, laughing Adarsh was always in and out of mischief. Invariably the first up the mango trees, forever ploughing through my anthurium beds and teasing the Labradors. He'd disappear into the servant quarters at the back of the house, playing endlessly with the children of the help, no matter how I cautioned about germs. Always the last to arrive at the dinner table, all the other children bathed and dressed, V tapping his fingers in irritation, tap tap tap-tap-tap. Just as the tension grew unbearable and I'd throw down my napkin to try and find him, in he would saunter, winking at his grandmother and ruffling Leela's hair. Beatings had no effect on the boy: all he had to do was look at me with those eyes, or smile his father's smile and my hand would falter. A fearless, exasperating, utterly charming child, with his mother wrapped firmly around his finger.

It wasn't just me. Almost everyone who met Adarsh fell a little in love with him and his easy, big-hearted ways. When we took them to Disneyland, I bought the children sunglasses. It was Adarsh who insisted I buy a pair each for the children of the help back home as well. 'They won't appreciate such things,' I said, but he'd have none of it.

How it made me laugh, when we returned to Basera, to see the gaggle of children, so different in appearance and upbringing, the cook's girls and the gardener's daughter, the boys of the maids and my four, all running around the back garden in identical, oversized Mickey Mouse eyewear.

**

The children grew, and we grew older. When oily Mishraji suggested that V contest the upcoming local elections, V scoffed at first. It was Adarsh who convinced his father otherwise. This was the missing link, he pointed out, not having a direct political handle on our myriad business interests. Instead of being at the mercy of this constant game of political musical chairs played by the unscrupulous, we needed a beachhead of our own.

V looked unconvinced.

'Think of all that you could get done, Dad!' Adarsh exclaimed. 'That overpass that has been lying half built for two years now, while the government installs inquiry commission after commission, the hospital wing that collapsed last month – those things would never happen under your watch.'

'Politics is a dirty game,' Daddy said dismissively.

'"Where the mind is without fear…"' I quoted softly.

'"Where the mind is without fear and the head is held high…"' Adarsh took up the poem, quoting effortlessly from Tagore's *Gitanjali*, the same lines I recited so often to him when he was a little boy. '"Where the clear stream of reason has not lost its way into the dreary sand of dead habit; Where the mind is led forward by thee into ever-widening thought and action… Into that heaven of freedom, my Father, let my country awake."'

I looked at my child as he stood there, shining with the idealism of youth, his voice ringing around the room. I saw in his eyes the image of my own father, as he must have looked at that age, fighting tirelessly for the freedom of this country.

❦

Despite Daddy's misgivings – or perhaps, precisely because of them – V decided to run for office. It was a long campaign, and we fought hard and clean, even as the opposition had us trailed by goons with loudspeakers, asking which self-respecting person would want to vote for someone who ate beef, someone whose own mother, *hai, hai, tauba*, smoked like a fish and drank like a man?

I was at V's side all the way, accompanying him from colony to basti, pallu drawn over my head as I talked of my freedom-fighter father, of the long-standing roots that both our families had in this state. Adarsh came with us as often as his school would allow. It made my heart ache with pride, to see him smile that infectious, effortless smile, handing out pencils and slates, and charming everyone in his orbit.

V might well have pulled it off except Mummy passed suddenly away. An aneurism, the doctor said. Just like that, she was gone, no fuss, no muss, an elegant end to an elegant life. V knelt beside her, caressing his mother's cheek, cradling her hand to his chest. We called the children home from school. They stood confused and disoriented, my heart turning over at the sight of Adarsh, the way his worried eyes were fixed unwaveringly upon his father. V noticed nobody, not any of us, the shuttered expression on his face warning us to stay away.

He pulled out of the elections. How I tried to dissuade him. Stay the course, finish what you started, have the conviction to see this through.

'Don't be disappointed,' Mishraji said later to me. He rolled a fresh paan and nodded his head at Adarsh. '*Hume usko dekha hua hain.* I watched him during the campaign.' He squeezed my arm, and I tried not to flinch. 'In some years, another Thakore on the *gadda*, who knows?'

⁕

V retreated into himself after that. Things turned for the worse between Daddy and him. Without Mummy's cool mediation, resentments from years ago came swirling to the surface. Mealtimes at Basera turned into sharp, unpleasant affairs, Daddy blundering through V's meticulously plotted minefields of sarcasm, no matter how much I tried to steer the conversation away.

V and I moved into separate bedrooms — so we could each sleep better, he said. I knew it was only to spare my feelings. I understood. I too had changed over the years. Firm flesh now ballooned in unexpected places, four pregnancies mapped in fine detail across once unblemished skin. After a certain age, how important is a physical connection anyway? It is the mental and emotional bonds between a husband and wife that carry you through your days. V loved me, in his own way.

I know he needed me.

❦

The children grew. Beanstalks four, spiralling upwards, our girls blossoming. Kishen got into Stanford. Adarsh had no interest in going abroad and had enrolled in the local university. I hadn't objected; it was better he stayed close, I told myself, learned the ropes of the business.

At the reception for the new governor, Mishraji pulled me aside. 'He's good,' he said, again standing just that smidge too close. 'Touch *hain uske paas*.' He rubbed his index finger against his thumb. '*Touch*. Rickshaw-wallahs or the rich – Adarsh can talk to any of them, same-to-same. Plus Thakore money backing… Party is keen. Strong future we see, for your boy.'

'Only thing is,' he continued, 'Party wants clean image. New India now, and we must have new faces. Clean. There is no *lafda* of drugs or anything, no?'

I laughed. 'No!'

He looked appraisingly at me. 'Girl trouble, drinking problem, gambling…'

I raised an eyebrow and he spread his hands placatingly, the gold rings flashing from his meaty fingers. 'Just checking, Garima. Party wants no *goondagiri*, no record of any sort. New, and clean.'

I looked over at where Adarsh was talking with a group of his friends. 'First, local,' Mishraji said. 'Municipal elections. Later, state.' Adarsh laughed, and turning his head caught my eye. He winked and raised his glass. *Minister Thakore.* It had a ring to it.

Mishraji squeezed my shoulder. 'Then who knows? All the way to the top, *haan*?'

I gave him my sweetest smile. '*Haan*, Mishraji,' I clinked my glass against his, 'to the top.'

❋

It was when we were preparing for Shanti's wedding that things went wrong. It was an excellent proposal, wealthy family, only two sons, and she was marrying the older boy. There was an air of excitement around Basera as lists of jewels and menus and invitees were feverishly drawn up. Adarsh teased his sister mercilessly, even V smiling at the constant banter. Stout, happy days with sunlight pouring through the house and flooding the garden, our home filled with music and young voices. When *it* happened, I was completely unprepared.

I was supervising the breakfast when Sundar, the gardener came asking for me. I sighed. Rheumy-eyed and belligerent, and prone to drinking besides, the only reason Sundar had lasted here as long as he had was because of his almost mystical touch with the flowers. 'The mouth of a sewer, the hands of a poet,' V would say of him whenever we had tea on the verandah, the garden spread before us in an undulating wave of colour.

Still, it was never easy dealing with Sundar. Instructing the cook to continue with the dosas, I went outside to where he was waiting, his daughter behind him. She'd practically grown up with my lot, a young girl about the age of my Leela. Pretty enough, after the fashion of her kind, slender and snub-nosed, with skin that shone like the night. I looked at her, at the way she stood, her eyes, red-rimmed and averted, and even before Sundar spoke, I knew. I just knew.

'Tell Memsaab what happened,' he said tersely. The girl started to cry. I shushed her and bundled them away to the privacy of V's study.

She was pregnant, the girl sobbed. It was Adarsh's. My palm swung of its own volition. I slapped her, and she cried harder. 'Please save me, Memsaab, you are my only hope.'

'See what your son has done to my daughter?' Sundar shouted. 'What will people say?'

My Adarsh, *my Adarsh*, the catch of this city, with girls throwing themselves left right and centre at him, sleeping with this lowly peasant? It could not be true, she was lying, the slut. I saw suddenly in my mind that long ago summer afternoon, all the children running about the garden in those ridiculous Mickey Mouse glasses. The bile rose in my throat.

I counted out two-thousand rupees from the safe, willing my hands to stop shaking as I thrust the money at Sundar. I warned them to keep their mouths shut, or else I would see them rot in jail. The girl started to cry again, saying she didn't want the money.

'Don't cry,' I said, patting her shoulder. I fought down my nausea. 'Haven't I known you since you were a little girl? You are a part of this household, I will do something, don't worry.'

❈

V looked at me expressionlessly as I told him, his face so empty of emotion that for a second I thought he mustn't have heard. 'Have you checked with Adarsh?' he asked.

We called him in to the study, but there was no need to ask. I knew, I already knew from the pit in my stomach.

'I'm sorry, Dad. I'm so sorry.'

V stood up. 'You'll sort this out, I trust,' he said to me, and walked out.

I stroked Adarsh's hair and this time, I could not stop my hands from shaking. 'Sshh. Quiet son, don't worry, I will do something.'

I carried on that day and the next as though nothing untoward had happened, supervising the goldsmith, visiting neighbours and family with V to personally hand out invites to the wedding. My head pounding as I smiled and accepted congratulations. How soon things would change if people knew.

I thought over and over of Mishraji. 'New face. Clean face.'

I called the girl to me, alone, without her nuisance of a father. Offered her any amount of money, to get her married, to get her a job, whatever she wanted, if she would abort the foetus. She started to cry again, babbling on about how much she loved Adarsh. She wanted the child.

She would not listen to reason, to neither my cajoling nor whatever veiled threats I managed to muster. In the end, there was nothing to do but go to Mishraji.

※※

If he was surprised to see me visit alone, he hid it well. 'Chai?' he asked, ordering two cups without waiting for my response and shutting the door after the tea had arrived.

I took a deep breath. 'There's a problem.'

He nodded sagely when I had finished. 'Problem,' he agreed. He came around to where I was sitting and touched a hand to my shoulder. 'But fixable.'

'I don't want this to ever surface again.'

He squeezed my shoulder. '*Haan*, of course. You did the right thing, Garima, coming to me.' He hesitated, and brushed his fingers lightly against my cheek. 'Could become a serious problem though. Party wants everything clean…' He stroked my cheek again.

I stayed very still. Looking him in the eye the whole time, I deliberately reached for his hand, and took his fingers in mine.

❧

Two days later, the girl disappeared. Just vanished, on her way home from the market. The police came to Basera. 'Routine investigation, Saar,' the inspector said apologetically to V as he slurped his tea.

What else can I tell you? That I paid Sundar three lakhs to leave Basera forever? That I warned him that if I saw him anywhere near the house, or heard one rumour, I would see that he came to a sorry end? That his eyes shone as he looked at the bundles of notes, even as he mumbled, 'Yes, Memsaab, yes Memsaab'? That V and Adarsh never even asked what happened?

That from the day, the very day that the girl went missing, that connection that my son and I shared, that invisible binding, it too disappeared? I love him just the same. Maybe more so, with every passing day, but I no longer can tell, even without turning around, when he walks in the door. No longer do I dream his dreams; I do not know any more what he is thinking, or what he feels.

Shanti's wedding was a grand affair. My daughter went with sixty-one saris and ten *tolas* of gold.

※※

We got all the children married. Daddy passed away. Slowly, painfully, riddled with cataract and arthritis, cursing God for making him suffer so. It finally ended one rainy afternoon as I was measuring out the rice for the cook. The maid came running, screaming for me. He was gone by the time I reached the bedroom.

V held stoic through the funeral, gracefully inclining his head, touching feet and accepting condolences from the never-ending crowds that had come to pay their respects. That night, he finally came to me. I held him and stroked his head as he cried, long shuddering sobs that soaked my nightgown. We slept in the same bed that night.

※※

All of this was years ago. Mishraji was as good as his word. Adarsh Thakore has become a name to be reckoned with. Like we knew all along, he has taken to 'ministergiri', as Mishraji puts it, like a fish to water. Adarsh has promised me that after I am gone, he will continue to perform the pooja at the local temple that I have been conducting each year since Shanti was married. He never asked who the pooja was for, and I didn't say.

He lives in Delhi now with his wife and children; I wait for their visits home.

I lie here, my joints swollen and useless, thinking back to all the times this house and I have seen. So many loved ones gone. Ma and Papa, two of my sisters, my brother Raja from a heart attack last year. Even unctuous old Mishraji, curling up and dying four winters ago. I am tired of these days that drag endlessly even as ghosts from the past wander in and out of the room.

I don't think of V as having died, how can I when I still feel him around me? I hear his voice in my ear – 'Garima, Garima…' Sometimes when I open my eyes from my sleep, I see him just disappearing around the door. I tucked his beloved letters into the folds of his shroud as he was placed on the bier. *'Go in peace my husband.'*

I know he waits for me.

My end is near though. I have had a new visitor. I woke with a start the other night, and saw her. A slight shifting of shadow, skin that blended into the dark. A young girl, the moonlight glinting from the rim of her endearing, oversized mouse-ear sunglasses.

I looked at the gardener's daughter, a calm in my heart. 'Yes, I know I did you wrong. I know the laws of karma, and that I will have to pay.'

'In my place, though, you might have done exactly the same.'

A finance professional by training, SARITA MANDANNA holds an MBA from the Wharton Business School, a PGDM from the Indian Institute of Management, and was most recently a private equity investor in New York. *Tiger Hills*, her debut novel, is a *New York Times* Editor's Choice, a TV Book Club pick in the UK and a *Globe and Mail* bestseller in Canada. Longlisted for the Man Asian Literary Prize, 2011, *Tiger Hills* is being translated into 14 languages worldwide.

The genesis of 'The Gardener's Daughter' lies in an actual incident that occurred some decades ago. A prominent local family, a wayward son, and a maid, suddenly poisoned. Nothing was ever proven, but rumours prevailed, and they all revolved around the matriarch of the family. If true, what could drive a mother to such extremes? What justification could she possibly allow? The story here is one exploration of that theme.

Amma and Her Beta

SHALINI SINHA

Motherhood dominates my thoughts in more ways than one as I set out to write about my son. Sitting with pen and paper, reminiscing about the birth of my child with special needs, it is in fact my own mother's memory looming large – initially in life, and then in death. In these past few months, I have fought fiercely for her life but, even as I did that, I was also gently preparing my son for her death. The irony of this has never felt more pronounced.

Today, I am not sure in whose voice I am speaking – as the mother of a special needs son, or the daughter of a terminally ill and recently deceased mother. Life and death, shun the neat little compartments we would like them to be contained in and now overwhelm me, churning and perforating all boundaries.

When, early in my life I had been presented with a reality which seemed harsh and unfair, it was she who stepped forward to embrace my pain and carry my burden. She did this all her life, giving me the space and the acumen to find happiness. My son added a strong new dimension to our mother–daughter relationship, binding us together in yet another bond, our shared love and concern for him.

My first memory of him is *her*, holding him in her arms, as she stood outside the delivery room, grinning from ear to ear, exclaiming, 'Look who has come into our lives!' My last memory of her is *him*, seventeen years later, poised and somber, thanking all those who had come for her prayer meeting.

That their lives were going to be intertwined was evident from the minute he was born; even as diagnosis after diagnosis of his disabilities came, her hold on him became stronger and fiercer, and his hold on her heart, invincible. Through the initial year of his existence, we had been gently and sometimes not so gently made aware of his many inherent disabilities. I remained a mute spectator in those early months – a little shocked, mostly numb and definitely not feeling any strong emotion for my son. Or that is what I thought.

My mother on the other hand was charged – she cared for him herself, with happiness, carried him around all the time, sang to him, never minded the long hours and difficult feeding arrangements, surrounding him with love and happiness and making many changes in her lifestyle and daily living to accommodate his needs. I remember asking her once, as she was singing a lullaby to him, 'What motivates you? How can you go on day after day, taking care of him, don't you fear what lies ahead?' She had looked at me for a split second, horrified at this very basic question from a new mother, and then had laughed softly, perhaps at my foolishness, and said, in Hindi, '*Ye to mera ansh hai*'. As she had carried on nonchalantly singing to him, I stared at her dumbfounded, speechless at the simplicity of her response. I

also saw in that moment her absolute acceptance of him –
no questions asked, no queries or quarrels, just a complete
and absolute acceptance into her heart and soul, and her
very being. 'He is a part of me,' she had said: nothing else
mattered!

My first lesson on motherhood came from my mother.

I have a very hazy recollection of the early years, and
even today when I look back it is through an emotional
fog. What I do recollect is the fear – an unknown but sharp
and cold fear of the future and what it held for us. My heart
ached and on most days, my chest was tight with anxiety,
as if a cold hand was pressing my heart. I was always by my
son, physically, but very rarely attended to him. My mother
remained his primary care taker.

While many professionals adopted various methods and
routes to make us aware of our son's condition, there wasn't
much clarity on what Down's Syndrome meant, in terms of
how it was to change our life. That it would change, for the
worse, was the underlying assumption in our interactions,
but 'how' was a question not many were ready to answer.
Many of these professionals were from the field of medicine
and hid behind abstract medical terms, inexplicable jargon
and abrupt and uncomfortable interactions. I felt a wave of
'pity' emanating from them (which, of course, I hated) and
an uncomfortable feeling that they somehow could see my
dismal future more clearly then I could. But I could never
ask what my future held – I was too scared of what their
answer would be.

Besides fear, a hunger dominated my being – hunger
for information and knowledge of what my son's condition

meant. I had very simple queries – will he recognise me? will he be able respond to me? In many ways I thought that perhaps if I knew what his future would be, I could then decide on my grieving patterns; formulate my life plans, and move ahead. Till then, I was living in limbo.

I was also struck, in those initial years, with my lack of exposure and knowledge about disability. However much I racked my brain, I could not remember reading anything beyond two lines in my school biology book on Down's Syndrome, in the chapter on genetics. These two lines, I could resuscitate from the folds of my memory with clarity, but not a word more. I also remembered nothing about interacting with any intellectually challenged person; I do not think I ever had. Three decades of my life had gone without any contact with this group of people, and I suddenly became aware of the invisibility of their lives. I was overcome with fear, of how my life would be (my grief still remained very selfish!) – not going out, not being accepted, having no support etc. With time, I started craving for more information on my son's condition – hearing parents' experiences, meeting children and adults with Down's – but I did not know where to look or whom to ask. The internet had not opened up our worlds at that time, unfortunately.

My husband and I remained close but also distant, drawing comfort from each other's presence but not sharing our grief. After all, what could he say to comfort me that I would not know would be a lie, and what happiness could I offer which was not forced? Our disappointment with what life had dealt out to us was evident to the other. We had no words of consolation to offer to each other in those early days. Our immediate families dealt with our crisis in their own ways, according to their individual personalities. Some maintained a distance, some offered false hopes, some hid behind philosophical and moral lectures but all spent many hours and lot of energy in discussions on why such a fate had fallen on us. Very few stood by us, and even fewer could step out of pitying us to give us real support. Our 'kismet' was the topic of many a drawing room conversation; we did not help matters, remaining aloof and prickly and absolutely unable to share or discuss our agony about our son's condition.

My son on the other hand defied the angst that surrounded him and flourished. He was a sweet baby and a very cute toddler, and reached most of his milestones just a few weeks behind. From the early months, he was holding his head up, following my mother's voice with his eyes, flinging his arms and legs in delight when my husband whistled. He had a very sweet smile – still does – and an extremely cheerful temperament. Soon he was crawling and uttering a few words. He loved water and my mother and he spent several hours together in an extended bathtime, which started with oil massage and sunbathing and ended with a long bath and a deep and invigorating nap. All these activities were personally performed by my mother, and bathtime remained a very special bonding time for them. She talked and sang to him incessantly, all of which he enjoyed with gleeful abandon. I have vivid memories of him, sitting in a red tub, with water up to his waist, a little wobbly, clutching the sides of the tub with both his hands and splashing away, chortling with delight.

The turning point came when we went abroad with my son, a year after his birth. I do not remember clearly what we wanted from this trip, definitely not a cure (that his condition was permanent had been conveyed to us many times), but surely some sort of solace or even escape. We also wanted to know about the therapies and the training opportunities available for our son. As a result, a good part of our stay was spent on visiting a genetic institute in the Mid-west. We got exposed to various assessment techniques, training mediums and methods and the world of paramedics – the speech, occupational and other therapists. But what we treasured most was the information – good reading material, access to special libraries, a social worker who was ready to deal with our queries at length. We also met parents and adults with Down's Syndrome, saw them being treated with dignity and respect, living independently, and leading lives that were both productive and meaningful. I remember our social worker had arranged for us to meet with a bunch of Down's Syndrome adults living independently, but we were never allowed to visit them – they were not to be 'exhibited'. We could, if we wanted, observe them in a mall while they did their weekly shopping but please could we be as discreet as possible and not stare too much. I was struck by the approach and the attitude, as much by the ability of these young and happy individuals; many things were crystalising in my mind.

We also visited another super specialist at Long Island in New York. The doctor's diary had been booked for months and she had specially taken out half an hour for us, after a long and pleading phone call from me to her assistant. It was a grey and drizzly day and unfortunately we arrived late, caught in the chaos of New York traffic and the ferry ride. Our first encounter with the doctor was intimidating to say the least. She was a tall lady, of Asian origin, with dramatic eye make-up, and a booming voice, and was quick to tell us off for arriving late. She made us sit in a large circle – she with her two assistants and nurses and us, and left my son to play in the middle. He was not given too many toys or aides but a large amount of space to crawl. She observed him closely as she talked – his gait, balance, attention span, response to tone and voice, eye-hand coordination. Occasionally, she changed places to observe him, while her team stimulated him – mildly, not overtly disturbing his self-play. Soon he was crawling around with energy, stopping to look up at people talking, making eye-contact and smiling, and then switching off from us to play his own game. The doctor looked through his medical papers but asked very few questions about my son. She seemed very interested in our lives – where we lived, how many people, who supported us. Her final prescription was dramatic. Take him back to India, she advised us, the Indian joint family is the best early intervention that you can give him, surround him with love and care. You are good parents, believe that. Find happiness for yourself and you will keep him happy!

My son also had an agenda while we travelled abroad, and that was to woo me! As we moved from one location to another, he adjusted well, enjoying himself and doing everything under the sun to win my heart. True to his personality, which would be evident much later, he did it with great subtlety. Ostensibly, he remained fixed to his father, but the child's intentions were very clear. In a crowded room, he would stop to catch my eye, and treat me with a beatific, heart-stopping smile and then ignore my mute requests for a repeat. He would quietly crawl up, sensing my quiet pensive mood and sit himself in my lap with a sly smile, as if fully aware of how my heart filled up with a fierce emotion for him, letting me feel both the pain and the joy of his presence in my life. He would climb all over me while I read a book and tried to play with my nose, ears, face, almost as if he wanted me to read him. In pain or fever, he would cuddle up and quieten as if my very touch soothed him. I soon found the numbness around my heart melting, and I began to derive great pleasure in his company. He enjoyed many things which stirred my soul. As I watched him chase the sunlight and shadows on the wall, I wondered how he was any different from any so-called normal child. He rain-danced and splashed in the pool, his love for water was evident from an early age. He danced to music, recognising his favourite song from the first note. He laughed with joy when the car jumped or went zig-zag and, like a true blue-blooded Bihari, he loved to eat *bhat*!

There is no doubt that information and knowledge gave us strength. Once I knew more about Down's Syndrome, it was as if my life changed. The future had hope and I could turn my life around. My husband and I were close again, our dedication and commitment in making a better life for ourselves had brought us together, as had our growing, fierce love for our only child.

We came back to India and, heeding the advice of the

New York doctor, started living with my parents. My father was a senior government bureaucrat and lived in a sprawling bungalow in a government colony. My son was surrounded by people – he went to walk the dog early in the morning and met the chowkidars, he sat in my father's official car, giggling, with his face pressed to the window while it was being cleaned and wiped, ran around in the sprawling garden with the gardener gathering the morning flowers, took his afternoon nap in the sun-dappled inner courtyard, while the bustle of a large household went on around him. His evenings were spent in the lush green front lawns, while my father drank tea and met friends and colleagues. My mother was his primary carer and he went with her everywhere – from ladies' parties to buying groceries. He was a happy child and she surrounded him with love and care, providing perhaps the best early intervention that he needed. He remained a cherished being in that household and by all who visited it. I had learnt another important lesson – most people around us take their clues from us, vis à vis our children. No doubt our children are the cynosure of many eyes in a social setting, but a lot of it can also be because of the vibes we send out.

He had a personality now, and though was not talking much, he could communicate with a few words, signs and facial expressions. But I still had many things to learn about inclusion and a funny incident comes to mind. One evening, my young cousin and I sat around in my aunt's living room, chatting away, while my son crawled around the room, playing. He had been bathed and fed and we looked forward to our hour of gossiping undisturbed. At some point, and unknown to us, my son had stopped playing and turned the living room upside down – all the books had been pushed from the table to the floor, the cushions and throws had been pulled down from the sofa, small show pieces had been removed from their places and a small fireplace (big for his size) had been overturned! All this he had been doing systematically and quietly, and I complained bitterly to my aunt about him. My aunt, much more perceptive than me, soon figured it out. She picked him up and sat him down where my cousin and I sprawled on the sofa. And for the next hour, he looked from me to her, giggling and laughing with us, while we took up discussing the dark secrets of our extended family once again. All he had wanted was to be included in our gossip session!

Essentially, my son changed us and our lives for the better, very rarely for the worse. I soon realised that life with a child with special needs can be a little solitary but need not be isolated. The society around has many people who want to reach out but do not know how, and if we were to create a space they would like to make a contribution to better our children's lives. This is in no way to belittle the apathy and discrimination that our children face – on the streets, in school, in public institutions – but also to acknowledge that things are also changing for the better. In the metropolitan cities, awareness about disability is increasing and many a time it is up to us to make that connection. Often, people start talking to him when they see us interacting with him normally, ruffle his hair, tweak his cheeks, or just make a friendly eye-contact. But they always look at us to help them take it forward – probably because they do not how to – and if, as parents and care takers, our vibes remain friendly and vibrant, they do strike a chord.

He continued to surprise us, with his abilities and his needs. When he ran for the Delhi Special Olympics, he defied my concern and anxiety, showing how much he needed such exposure in his life. As I saw him on the track, sprinting, with the wind in his hair, I was awestruck by the sheer joy on his face. He was running for the pleasure of it, an award was far from his mind. When I saw him perform on the stage, it was again that joy of participation and of being given an opportunity.

And I owe it to my mother who was quick to point out that the problem was not in his lack of ability but in our lack of aspirations for him. She urged us to discover and develop the best opportunities for him as he grew. A graceful and giving person, it was as if she had found her calling in him. She was quick to form a rapport with young special educators who worked with him, many called her 'amma', and enjoyed the *nashta* that she cooked for them and the sweaters that she knitted for their children. But her heart remained with the special mothers: she never needed words to understand the deep dichotomies that tore at our lives or the small pleasures that elevated our souls. In a true 'amma' way, she just felt them like we did! I saw her, on many occasions, quietly offering support and advice to other mothers, forming life-long and nurturing relationships with them and their children.

Even as he came close to me, my son remained very tied to my mother. I was the disciplinarian (which he resented as he entered his teens), but with her, it remained a touching of the souls. It is not as if our journey has always been smooth, there were many set-backs too – his inability to cope in a normal school, our inability to find quality services, his teenage angst – and in each she remained the strongest, in spirit and in her faith in him. As she grew old, she became a less hands-on mother for him but remained his truest well-wisher and supporter. Prodding us to make roads where none existed, she urged us to find ways and means of enriching his being, making all kinds of sacrifices in her personal life in order to give him a meaningful future. When he needed to go to a vocational centre thirty miles from our home, she took the responsibility of making the two-hour trip each day with him.

When she was diagnosed with cancer, my mother was devastated with the unfairness of it. She had committed herself to taking care of her grandson and was angry that her mission was being cut short. It took her a long time to come to terms with the inevitable, and her inability to change it. And yet through her illness and long drawn-out treatment, her primary concern was him – she stocked her hospital fridge with his favourite drink, so that I could carry it with me on the days that I went directly from the hospital to pick him up. She enquired about him every day, sometimes even in the midst of drug-induced delirium: has he come back from school, who is looking after him, why have we all left him alone at home? But she never allowed him to visit her, determined as she was to not expose him to the anxiety and grief of a hospital visit and a terminally ill patient. Her own deep longing for him remained contained within, even death could not make her put her own needs before his.

As for my son, by the time she fell ill, he was a teenager and had in some sense 'outgrown' her, spending more time with his father and me. He had his school and social life. But the deep bond with her remained, became deeper during the illness, evident in small interactions on the days that she was at home – he often went to her with imaginary pains and aches and even as she was wracked by the all-consuming cancer pain, she would sit up to apply a cream or a pain balm for him and give him a special healing kiss. He went away, loving the attention, and it seemed as if, miraculously, her pains too receded for a bit. In the first round of cancer, all of us wanted to protect him from the harshness of the disease and its treatment. Taking his cue from us, he withdrew from her, and in retrospect I feel we did a great injustice, both to him and to her. He found it difficult to cope with her loss of hair, being bed-ridden and frequent trips to the hospital, and almost pretended he did not see. She had always worn a sari, he bitterly complained about her wearing a nightie now. Once she recovered and was back on her feet, it was as if he had a new lease on life.

When the cancer came back the second time, a few months later, we decided to include him, rather than exclude him in our fight. He dealt with it very bravely and did us proud, cooperating with us in many small and big adjustments that we had to make. In her final passing, he and I were joined together again in our grief, the vacuum in our lives impossible to articulate. I saw him lying awake on many a night, tearless but sad, tossing and turning, trying to make sense of his loss, not saying much. And then it had burst forth, in a quiet whisper, deep into one such night of insomnia. 'Why did Amma die?' A profound question, asked in all innocence, but not very different from the torment that raged in my own heart. If he found it difficult to come to terms with the finality of death, so did I. He could not believe she had left him, I could not believe that she could. And both us draw solace from what a friend, also a mother of a special needs son, told me, 'She could have left you and me, but not our children. Do you believe she could ever leave them? Never! She is here, with him, in him...'

SHALINI SINHA works as an independent consultant on gender and developmental issues and is based in New Delhi. She has considerable experience in developing, formulating and evaluating gender-related, community-based development projects, for the South Asia region and has worked with international donors, NGOs and women's organisations. She was introduced to the world of disability by her son, and like Alice in Wonderland, she has found the journey both disturbing and charming; angst-ridden and laced with humour; challenging and inspiring. Deeply committed to creating a world where her son and his friends find dignity and visibility, Shalini Sinha's current affiliations are with Muskaan, a support group of parents with special needs children, specialising in addressing issues around vocational training and employment for adolescents and adults with special needs.

Selected Poems

TISHANI DOSHI

The Day After the Death of My Imaginary Child

Is a moment in the doorway
of an underground cave
with paintings of bright buffalo,
pinpricks of rain.
It's when the spider of dream
that's been shadowing me
since I bled my way to womanhood
whispers again,
how I'll outlive any child
I could hope to bear,
for thinking that a body
made of sand and water
could dare to make one of silver.

The day after the death
of my imaginary child
is a day I count separately
like a resolute wave
spewing up finger-pink
birthmarks, tips of brooding,

foamy hair. It's knowing
that at the end
there'll be the same brush
of swallow, spit, sudden light.
I'll be asked to spend myself
over molecule of son or daughter —
take all that failed infinity
of body, fibre, blood
and surrender it as harvest
to the seasons of the famished sea.

The Deliverer

Our Lady of the Light Convent, Kerala

The sister here is telling my mother
how she came to collect children
because they were crippled or dark or girls.

Found naked in the streets,
covered in garbage, stuffed in bags,
abandoned at their doorstep.

One of them was dug up by a dog,
thinking the head barely poking above the ground
was bone or wood, something to chew.

This is the one my mother will bring.

❊

Milwaukee Airport, USA

The parents wait at the gates.
They are American so they know about ceremony
and tradition, about doing things right.

They haven't seen or touched her yet.
don't know of her fetish for plucking hair off hands,
or how her mother tried to bury her.

But they are crying.
We couldn't stop crying, my mother said,
feeling the strangeness of her empty arms.

❊

This girl grows up on video tapes,
sees how she's passed from woman
to woman. She returns to twilight corners,

to the day of her birth.
How it happens in some desolate hut
outside village boundaries

where mothers go to squeeze out life,
watch body slither out from body,

feel for penis or no penis,
toss the baby to the heap of others,

trudge home to lie down for their men again.

Undertow

I

I hold my husband in plastic bags.
He's whispering like a soft, worn thing,
Drop me here, drop me gently.

Everything is terribly light — incense,
ash, the thinness of his voice falling
into waves, disappearing.

II

The sea picks up my life,
empties it across itself.
I see it spilling over, dissolving.
Here are the forgotten parts —
A pink night sky, broken bangles,
a fisherman walking away from the light.

There you are, held up with wind and sails.
If you would turn, you would hear me say,
Come back, my arms ache from all the carrying.
Underneath, you're lost in a place
where everything is scraped together
and nothing is thrown back.

You sink. Colours dissolve.
You move hair from your forehead,
salt from your eyes. You're left with greys —
calling out to me, bubbles

instead of words. It is a silent death:
one I feel before it happens.

III

Was there a child then? The child I could not have?
With hair that shakes and shines as though a sun
were gleaming under her roots. I want to stroke her.

Lean over and touch her. *Come here, let me hold you.*
I want only daughters — a thick rope of black
around her neck. She calls; the beginning of your name.

If I were really a mother, I would do it quick
and painless, out of love. Take the hair —
twist, yank, drop; tilt her over like a bag of sand.

It would be done then. There would be less
to clean up. She will never be like me.
The death of her child will kill her.

IV

If you must collect pictures, take them
when I'm looking away. Here's a beach again —
the nets spread on the sand drying,
A fish in the corner slapping its tail.

Nothing matters then,
We'll meet when we're warm and dry.
Take this picture — my shoulders, the bone,
the shine, the criss-cross of white straps.

V

I'm eight years old, running into the sea.
Run in, my mother says, *Go on then like a naked girl.*
Nobody cares, nobody's watching.

The sea pulls me in around the ankles,
grabs the sand from underneath, shows me
a glimpse of my life, what it will be like later.

It was all calm once, long ago, a teardrop
between apartment buildings. But here in my life;
Hiss hiss. This one is no good.

This one doesn't love you.
This one doesn't know what you need.
Leave, let go, stop.

The frothy fingers at my throat,
the voice pouring into me,
a terrace of vanishing blue.

You will leave this one.
You will leave this place.
For a while you will know nothing.

That Woman

That woman is here again.
She's found her way out
from under the stairs.
For centuries she's been weeping
a song about lost men,
the disappearance of beauty,
                    disgrace.
Now she's back in the world,
down by the traffic lights,
in the shade of trees,
hurrying to the parlour
to fix the crack in her face.

Don't become that woman,
my mother said.
By which she meant,
don't become that woman
who doesn't marry
            or bear children.
That woman who spreads her legs,
who is beaten, who cannot hold
her grief or her drink.
Don't become that woman.

But that woman and I
have been moving together
                for years,
like a pair of birds
skimming the surface of water,

always close to the soft
madness of coming undone;
the dark undersides of our bodies
        indistinguishable
from our reflections.

The River of Girls

i.m. India's missing girls

This is not really myth or secret.
This murmur in the mouth
of the mountain where the sound
of rain is born. This surging
past pilgrim town and village well.
This coin-thin vagina
and acid stain of bone.
This doctor with his rusty tools,
this street cleaner, this mother
laying down the bloody offerings
of birth. This is not the cry
of a beginning, or a river
buried in the bowels of the earth.
This is the sound of ten million girls
singing of a time in the universe
when they were born with tigers
breathing between their thighs;
when they set out for battle
with all three eyes on fire,
their golden breasts held high
like weapons to the sky.

TISHANI DOSHI was born in Madras, India, in 1975. She graduated with a Masters degree in writing from the Johns Hopkins University and worked in London in advertising before returning to India in 2001, where an encounter with the choreographer Chandralekha led her into an unexpected career in dance. Doshi has published two books of poetry and a novel – all of whom she considers her children. Her next child is a novella called *Fountainville*. For more information, please visit www.tishanidoshi.com.

The First Cry

SHINIE ANTONY

Years of hoping against hope had caught up with her. She stopped timing her ovulation and in the main seemed to be accepting a childless fate. She no longer inflicted tests or that high keening cry on her husband and appeared to give up, as he had been telling her to all along.

Sophie, he had told her many times during their decade of desperate dreaming, be sensible. And it was as if she opted for sense with a vengeance.

'We have no children,' she took to confiding casually in strangers on trains or flights, more out of a compelling need to believe it herself and forfeit the urge for miracles.

'Children none,' Sophie declared with a regal tilt to head, as if entering a land for the barren. A password not for her own arrival anywhere but to point out exits for whoever may find it embarrassing or offensive that here was she, infertile, non-incubating, hatching nothing and no one in nine months from now.

No children, she said in a careful little voice. Without inflection, vowels abrupt, so that it sounded, before the ear may decode all of it, like a word of foreign origin. 'Nchldrn-nchldrn' to anyone who'd listen, before they even asked, for she wanted it out of the way, the matter of offspring, their age, school and gender.

When someone offered a puppy on her birthday, she said briskly, 'No, thank you,' patting the pup as if to behead it. And the guest had no choice but to hold on to his gift – who had vacated its bow-tied straw basket early on – even while eating cake.

Which was a far cry from her staring at a sunlit spot in their home for hours, saying as evening fell, 'It was kind of lavender.'

Truth to tell, a kind of exhaustion had crept over them. That and the memory of the 'honeymoon baby' they almost had in the first year of their marriage, about whom they had said with careless vanity, 'this is too early, so unplanned.' The one who got away because of an imperfect heart that the doctors detected soon enough with their sophisticated weaponry. They had twisted and turned to this doc and that, asking, asking, but all agreed on the need to abort. 'There will be other babies,' was what they said. And Sophie had asked him, her husband, 'Yes, there will be others, but what about this one?'

She had stayed overnight in the hospital, worn a regulation open-backed gown, and plucked at the labour-inducing drip on her arm. The nurses asked her, quite kindly, if she wanted to see it, hold it, the baby with a heart that wouldn't beat. And though Sophie had felt a fluttery brush on her inner thigh – a finger? a palm? – she refused to turn sentimental over the baby who did not make her a mother. She shook her head and the nurses went away with what should have been the apple of her eye.

Then it had begun, the copulation by clock and calendar, the long vigil, the medical onslaught, two feet propped up on a pillow all night, novenas in an out-of-the-way church, nonstop advice from well-wishers, the growing hush deep within her body... Marching in missionary position in the battlefield of their bed month after month, night after night, for ten long years. Left-right-left.

'Why don't you adopt?' Sophie's mother asked just recently on Skype.

Susheel had looked at Sophie, too, to gauge her reaction. But with her new no-nonsense air, she said, 'Mommy, give us time to catch our breath.'

It had been traumatic, he silently agreed, but more for her than him. He watched her warily a while for any covert hysteria, but all minor forms of fishwifery were explicable from here on.

And, she added to him in a tone approaching cheer, there is enough time; she was only thirty-five years old. She began to make travel plans, to forward elaborate maps, charts and flight schedules to him, to call up people they knew and ask them, liltingly, about the weather in a certain place and suitable clothes. That summer they were going to go away, just the two of them, to some secret destination and discover what they were when just by themselves, without this constant hum in the ear, this expectation of another.

To that end came her general cry of 'We have no kids!' like an unseen amputation or something shot pointblank in air. It was the deliberate manufacturing of another mood.

It was around then that the pregnancy took them unawares. There were no warning signs. The absence of her periods they'd attributed to the regular hormonal injections she used to take earlier to boost her fertility, her nausea was something she ate – 'the prawns,' she grumbled, retching into the bathroom basin – and the pale anaemic air they put down to the clammy weather and her general weakness.

It was only in her fourth month that a routine blood test drove them clean out of their minds.

He had come home clutching the report, his face unable to manage any expression. She took one look at him and sensed doom. 'I am dying,' she thought. 'I am dying and he doesn't know how to tell me. I have damaged myself beyond repair with my invasions of my own body. One should never try to have and to hold what one cannot,' she was thinking when he handed her the report.

The word danced before her eyes. *Positive*. Positive what? Then she scanned the word overleaf: pregnancy. She sat with a painful thud on the dining table chair, the flat dark wood jarring the base of her spine.

From then on the two of them did everything in their power to drive each other, if possible, even more mad. Sleep, he'd order when she wanted to eat *nei*-roast dosa made in an unhygienic roadside handcart three kilometers from home. Walk, he'd nudge her when sleep smote her down senseless. Most of all she wanted sugarcane juice; to smell, drink, take a shower in it. And he brought her bottles and bottles of it till her blood sugar shot through the roof and distracted with gestational diabetes.

The foetal heartbeat rhymed with all those beeping machines, but still they ran around, headless chicks, for more tests. 'No, no,' they were shooed off. 'Everything is fine. Nothing to worry.'

Sophie and Susheel rarely let the other finish a sentence for fear of it lapsing into… Instead, they kept in the limelight his clients, the day's headlines, her bowel movement. Non-aligned words, at room temperature. Any reference to due date was reluctant, of the necessary kind, after a scan or when nightmares split the back of her head. Silence was a tacit talisman. Sometimes he pressed his lips urgently to the nape of her neck and she understood.

Accomplices, they kept the 'good news' to themselves. No point telling her mother or his sister, who would all just worry incessantly, phone constantly or arrive instantly. Off they'd go, loved ones, bumpity-bumpity-bump down some staircase, dragging him and especially her by the hand. No, when it came to stark raving mad they were doing fine on their own. The floppy state of the bedroom, the chaos in the kitchen, the sheer nervous fizz making soda of their blood were proof enough of their own mental displacement.

She began to hyperventilate. This is god's child, she said. Nothing else, she felt, could explain this magic. At another time, forgetting about angels flapping about her room with celestial messages, she'd proclaim it the devil's own sperm.

'Take it out or it will kill me,' she yelled at midnight, louder and louder until mildly sedated.

'I am having triplets or at least twins!' She snatched his hand and put it on her belly. 'Now you can hear them breathe, can't you?'

Oh, go to sleep, he said.

He couldn't pamper her every day. His job – he was a lawyer – was enough complication and he should not take too seriously what his inner voice whispered to him were merely 'feminine' fears. He had to conserve his strength for later. One had to get through this, the interminable dullness of the waiting room. He hoped to hell the third trimester would end earlier than indicated. His friend's wife, who was Sophie's obstetrician, had winked the last time they met, 'Pick out an auspicious moment, choose any star, Avittam or Thiruvadira, and we'll take the baby out that day.' Apparently, horoscopes were negotiable.

Sobbing piteously one Sunday after Mass, Sophie told him her mind was tricking her into wanting 'only bad things' for the baby. 'Make my mind go blank,' she pleaded. 'How can I want my baby to be anything but perfect? I throw him down cliffs and put him under the wheels of a truck. I am a bad mother. I can't be mother at all…'

She knew hundred percent that when the time came and they cut her open, they'd find a) nothing, b) a monster with two horns and a tail, c) a stuffed toy, d) a foetus dunked face-down in its own amniotic fluid.

Option d, click-clicked a tongue in her head, option d. Insomnia was her ally against sanity and Susheel, who said many things in many tenors to her, from sweet nothings to fuck off, that made sense to her only as and when they were being said.

The surety that enemies were plotting against her tied her stomach in knots. The doctors were lying, there was no baby, and if there was one, it had no head, no heart. Her own physical misshapenness, that all called fleeting, was taking its toll. She caught sight of her bump in mirrors, in shop windows, but never looked at it directly if she could help it. Didn't want to *see* what was inside her, speckled, the colour of espresso, with a gooey centre. *See* and self-detonate.

She took to flushing the folic acid, the calcium pills, vitamin this, vitamin that down the toilet. Who knew what was in that? Whom could she trust? Whom could she turn to? Best, she decided in a moment of fatigue, to pretend faith in her husband, for there were long intervals when he seemed to her the villain of the piece.

When the time came and her salwar was drenched, they both, without a fuss, drove to the hospital in a flash. Above all, they did not want to hope, or at least let on to each other that they were hoping such hopes where all hopes led to one hope:

Just live. Make it out of there into here. Please.

As the labour intensified, he sat down next to her and the two of them said nothing, not a thing. Their mouths were dry and ears clogged.

'One baby coming up!' said the doctor merrily.

A muted *huh-huh-huh* wisped out of nowhere, soft, offended.

'A boy,' said someone to someone else. Then silence.

Sophie lay back, convinced that nothing was right. She watched with droopy eyes a nurse walk over to Susheel and hand him...

'What is it?' she asked with a return of panic.

He shook his head and bent over her, to place in her

arms… She trembled once violently, as if to stop him. Wary and numb she looked down then with the slowest of eyes.

A microscopic nose, tangled lashes, skin too loose to fit yet. She breathed out in a whoosh, though she knew it was rash to think everything fine. She was yet to meet his eyes, count his toes, feel the pulse in that diaphanous wrist.

She would have thrown her head back and laughed loudly – for she knew instinctively that she would have wanted to laugh at this point – but could feel neither her head nor neck or, for that matter, was unsure of working up a smile, let alone a laugh. Her very skin seemed to be turning inside out this minute, ripping inarticulately from the back of her to the front.

In the last eleven years, Sophie had rehearsed many words with which she would welcome a child of hers into the world but now, to be honest, all of language was a sob in her chest. She thought, lucidly enough, 'But I don't even know you,' and burst into tears.

Shinie Antony has written two novels, two short story collections and compiled two anthologies – *Kerala, Kerala, Quite Contrary* and *Why We Don't Talk*. While her first book, *Barefoot and Pregnant* (2003), explores dysfunctional motherhood, her novel *When Mira Went Forth and Multiplied* (2011) revolves around a fake pregnancy. A mother of two, all she asks for in life is an afternoon nap.

The Slap Flies Off My Hand

Prabha Walker

The hospital room was once a lovely lime green. Age has turned it the colour of goose shit. It is not an unpleasant space, however. A picture of Mont Saint Michel on one wall, blown up cartoons by Plantu on another. They were funny to begin with. Now we hardly notice them.

It's another scorching Paris summer, baking hot outside, over 40°C, with old people dying in droves. We huddle together in our blue hospital gowns, grumbling and complaining, the windows wide open, hardly noticing the chemical stench of our sweat. We all smell the same. We wouldn't know any better, would we?

There are five of us in the group, all undergoing chemotherapy for one form of cancer or another; all trying to come to grips with constant nausea, peeling skin, burning stomachs, sore-riddled mouths and egg-like heads; all doing battle with our inner demons. Sans eyebrows, sans eyelashes, our scalps smooth as stones worn down by the river. With the exception of Ania who is football-fat, we are rickety, stick-thin – sere driftwood washed ashore. My Indian skin has turned a jaundiced yellow. Theirs the colour of curdled milk.

Our therapy group meets every week. It's been six months now and we have bonded. Perhaps out of necessity, but more, I feel, out of genuine empathy. Beautiful Eloise whose hollow cheeks give her a Nefertiti look, intellectual, tolerant, good-tempered Ania whom we call Ania Lasagna, rich, lazy and vituperative Florence, tortured Dominique and me, the little Indian mouse with the large, loopy eyes.

Ania looks ill, puffy and bloated like a sow. She is off chemo and back on cortisone and morphine which means she may not have long to go. But before she kicks it she wants to write a book, she says, detailing all this useless suffering. Her legal practice will be looked after by her friend. But what will happen to her boy? There was never a father to start with. One by one she makes us promise we will look after him. Christophe, who has taken to signing his name Xtof, is thirteen; rebellious, angry, frightened and bewildered by what is happening to his mother.

Florence is worried her husband is having it off with the maid. He's going to ditch her. He tells her quite bluntly she's an unbearable nag who complains, smells, looks ill and has lost her hair. 'That little slut,' she says, describing the new *bonne*. 'She's efficient, I'll grant, all bobs and curtsies, Madame this and Madame that. But I know she'll be on him the moment my back's turned. I must get her out before the end of the week.' We all find Amelie pleasant and solicitous but Florence has sacked four maids since we have known her. She is terrified she'll find herself out in the street after Henri swans off with the latest addition to their domestic staff – the rest are all males, of course. 'It cannot happen. It will not happen. Henri is not like that,' we tell her. 'He's devious. These over-pious Catholics are all like that,' she says and of course there's no convincing her.

Eloise amuses us all. She has brought along a special little valise full of the trinkets she bought since we last met a week ago and she pulls them out one by one like a magician: 1930s turbans, flowing retro cocktail robes, strings of pearls and a variety of wigs. She blew her bank, spent thirty-thousand euros in half an hour, she says. 'I felt better for the rest of the evening. And now I want all of you to feel good too.' There are presents for each of us. An XXL maternity robe for Ania, modelled to peals of laughter. History books for Dominique, a bottle of Eau de Mere for Florence's skin that has taken to bursting out in ugly red rashes and some lovely tea from Mariage Frères for me. 'Here, you can drink all the cat piss you want,' she tells me laughing.

I like them all. They have taken me into their midst, their 'little Indian mouse' who speaks poor French, has just been dumped by her boyfriend and is all alone in this world. But it is for sullen, withdrawn Dominique that my heart beats the most. She worries me, attracts me, irritates and fascinates me. She is rail-thin with a pointy chin and sharp nose, not what you would call a conventional beauty. But her eyes, blue as the deepest ocean with a sparkle all their own, her wit, her intelligence, her ambition, even her belligerence have me in thrall.

Today she is puffy-eyed and dulled by weeping. I do not need to ask what the matter is. I know. I have known ever since I first met her just before Christmas last year. Howsoever reluctantly, I have become her mother-confessor.

Dominique hits her small son Eric without quite knowing why and then she is gnawed by guilt and self-loathing. He is four now, a curiously dysfunctional child, hyperactive, touching everything in sight, fidgety, incapable of joining a playgroup. Early pictures show him as a chubby baby with a mass of wild curls and a happy smile that connects with the world.

And yet, his mother hits him and has done so since he was a year old. Why?

'I think I was depressed. Post-partum blues perhaps? I hadn't wanted a child. I was having a terrific time meeting new people, making friends. I'm not from a great big bourgeois family like Pascal. My origins are grotty, small town, working class: I wanted to leave that behind. It was Pascal who wanted fatherhood. But when the baby came he did absolutely nothing. 'An infant that small is just like a vegetable. They become interesting at around five,' he said.

'I was working but I didn't have a full-time job when Eric was conceived. I had to go back to work six weeks on the dot after he was born or I would have lost my place. The birth was difficult. There was some foetal stress. And when I came home there was just masses of work – bottles to be washed, nappies changed, the house cleaned. And Pascal just let me get on with it. No time for the baby, the house or for me. HE wanted the child and I had to give up a life that I LOVED,' she says. 'I think I hated Pascal for what happened and I took it out on Eric instead. And it happened that way because if I had spit venom at Pascal, he would have turned around and left. So Eric literally became the whipping boy.'

Dominique loves little Eric more than life itself. And yet she nags and scolds him constantly. She wants him to be perfectly obedient, better, smarter, cleverer than the other little ones in his playschool. Because that's how she wants to be in life – smartest, cleverest, best.

'I know what I do is horrible, that it does not bear contemplating. Here I am, denouncing human rights abuses in my articles and broadcasts and beating up my child in the same breath. I know I am doing wrong and yet I cannot seem to stop. The slap flies off my hand before I can pause to think. I have tried psychiatry. Don't think I haven't. I'm fully aware of the harm I cause. To him, to me. I am destroying us both. And yet, I cannot seem to stop. You are the only person I can talk to. Perhaps because you are foreign. You don't know our set-up so you don't judge me. With your Indian wisdom I know you understand that I don't want any of this to happen,' she tells me over and over again. I am not sure I am prepared to don this role or that I'm very good at helping her. All I can do is to listen and reassure.

She met her husband, Pascal, when they were both studying at the university of Nanterre near Paris. He was training to be a lawyer. She had her heart set on journalism and joined the prestigious CPJ in Paris, while he became an articled junior. It was all part of the overall grand scheme, for although it was assumed Pascal would one day inherit his father's practice in Bordeaux, he was at odds with his family and wanted to make his own way in life. Their first three years together were wonderful. They lived it up. She was mad, irreverent, out to have a good time. He was high-spirited, unconventional. They made a perfect couple. She got a job working the graveyard shift at a newspaper. He floated his own fledgling legal firm.

And then Dominique discovered she was pregnant. The nausea was dreadful. But they needed the second salary so she dragged herself to work every night, not daring to declare her pregnancy for fear of losing her temporary job. She would leave home at 8pm and return exhausted at 2am. Their social life dried up. Pascal began going out alone with his buddies. Suddenly everything changed.

'I hated being pregnant, dreaded the birth. Pascal never joined the pre-natal classes. Suddenly he had changed from being this delicious fun-loving husband to a depressing, bourgeois prig. He worked very hard, I admit. It was just the wrong time, I think. His law firm was young. My job was not permanent. That put a lot of pressure on both of us. But instead of shouldering the burden equally, he just shrugged it off saying, 'that's women's work. If I work so hard, it's for the family.' How anachronistic was that? I too had ambition.

'Why is it so bad not to have the maternal instinct? Why have women been forced into the caretaker's role? Just because they ovulate, carry the child, give birth and produce breast milk? I find the blood and guts of birthing repulsive. I dislike the thought that I must "suckle my young." And yet I love my child with a deep, enduring love. I did not wish to spend all my days cooing at him and smelling of breast milk. I needed my career, needed to read and think, use my brains. I needed to LIVE.'

Dominique's *cri de coeur* came a full ten years before Elizabeth Badinter in her hugely criticised book *The Conflict:*

How Modern Motherhood Undermines the Status of Women. In an interview with *The New Yorker* in 2012, Badinter declared, 'Motherhood is a choice, not an obligation. When you have a child, you become a mother. But you're not JUST a mother. When one is a mother, life does not stop. To be just a mother is not to be a fully realised woman. It's one part of your life, not your whole life. I find that liberating. I don't want to start sending children off to wetnurses again, but I think that some part of that break between the child and the mother works very well for me and I'd like to conserve that. My advice to young women would be: don't give up your job. Don't ever give up your economic independence. You must be able to survive without a man. Because if you no longer get along with your partner or he treats you badly and you don't have the means to leave him, you're enslaved.'

It is ten years since that hospital afternoon in 2002 when five women, four French, one Indian, spent hours talking together. Ania did write her book before she died a year later. It has since been made into a film. Xtof, as we fondly call him, is now twenty-three and has three adoptive mothers looking over his shoulder, encouraging him.

Florence too is no longer with us. She died by her own hand a year after Henri set up house with Amélie. She was right after all – the maid got him in the end.

The cancer ended Eloise's professional dancing career but she teaches ballet at a school attached to the Opéra de Rouen.

I have lived to tell the tale and so has Dominique who is no longer abusive but has managed to establish a reasonable relationship with Eric. By that I mean as stable as possible, given the circumstances. For that she had to leave Pascal, send Eric to a boarding school and undergo intensive therapy. She is a successful broadcaster and lives for her work.

'I still ask myself why I was abusive. Part of the explanation of course, is that I was slapped around by my mother as a child. But that's not enough. I continue to be consumed by guilt although Eric and I have tried to resolve our problems through joint therapy sessions. I think leaving Pascal and finding my feet without him as a crutch was crucial. He appeared modern but in fact, he was very old-fashioned and paternalistic. So I allowed myself to be pushed into the traditional maternal role. I hated him for it and I hated Eric for being the cause of my "condition". Once I had walked out, Eric was my sole responsibility and I found myself assuming it all. I think my cancer was self-induced, a product of guilt.'

Dominique's explanation sounds too pat to my ears. I know she is consumed by her work and her son resents her for it. Keeping him away from her in boarding school was one way of protecting him from the destructive forces of her ambition. Eric was small, helpless and needy. She could not ignore him without feeling terrible guilt. But her anger at his constant, crying, needy presence led her to lash out at him, push him away, punish him and herself at every turn even though she loved him. What she wanted was for him to leave her in peace when she was editing or writing one of her radio biographies that later made her so famous. But Eric is stubborn like his mother. He has never really ceased to demand what he considers his due: his mother's love and attention.

The peace between them remains tenuous. Even now sometimes, when she puts out a hand to stroke Eric, he flinches, anticipating a slap instead. That hurts them both. She realises she can never undo the damage she has caused and he is ashamed for both of them because he understands how desperate she is to make amends, that the outstretched hand no longer intends to inflict pain.

That said, like all abused children, Eric has learnt to tread carefully and make do with little. He respects her workspace and is inordinately proud of his mother who looks like a teenager and is recognised by people in the street. It gives him a certain cachet with his friends and he likes the fact that their grand apartment is often host to politicians, actors and other celebs. But once in a while he finds a terrifying rage engulfing him and he has a history of broken relationships.

Dominique is learning to better control herself. Fame, position and a comfortable income have calmed her insecurity about her origins and her worth. She has acquired poise and a degree of equanimity. She continues to see her cancer as 'the price' she had to pay for her 'wickedness' for there is a deep strain of old-fashioned morality running through her, although she would deny it if confronted.

Step after small step, they have tried to extricate themselves from the blind anger and violence that holds fast their past. Theirs will never be a truly easy or happy relationship: they skated for too long on shifting sands and terrifying memories prevent them from building something with a solid foundation. But they care for each other. And hold on to each other. And perhaps that's as far they will ever be able to go.

PRABHA WALKER is an Indian living in Paris. She has done extensive research on domestic violence in Europe, including conjugal violence in France, Spain and Switzerland.

Kunti

NAMITA GOKHALE

All my sons loved me, in their different ways. Yudhisthira, seed of Dharma, the god of righteousness, was born on the eighth hour of the day, when the moon was in conjunction with the constellation of Abhijit. My second son, Yudhisthira, eldest of the Pandavas, embodiment of virtue. Mighty-armed Bhima, born of the wind god Vayu, fell from my lap the day he was born, shattering into a hundred fragments the hilltop where I was resting. I remember the day well: it was the day Gandhari gave birth to Duryodhana.

Yudhisthira's virtue, Bhima's strength. Then, my valorous son Arjuna, the brave and invincible seed of Indra. I loved him the most. My sons Nakula and Sahadeva, brave, righteous and beautiful, born of the immortal Ashwins from the womb of my co-wife Madri.

I have known the love of gods and divine beings—five of them. Durvasa's bitter blessing brought glory to Pandu's line. But I never knew the love of my husband. He never fondled my breasts or stoked my joys in the conjugal bed. It was Madri after whom he lusted, always, with his impotent body and hungry spirit. I was his lawful wife, but all he wanted from me was heirs, kings to wear the crowns of conquest, warriors to sacrifice in battle.

'Go to a learned brahmana,' he would say. 'There is no sin in seeking out a rishi and requesting him to interrupt his austerities. No, I shall not be jealous.'

I told him of the boon that Durvasa had granted me. His eyes slanted with surprise, with subverted lust. Together, we summoned the gods, one after the other, and I took their seed. But I never told Pandu of how, when I was young, the Sun god had shown me his radiance and I had belonged to him alone.

I look back on that time when I was a young girl as though it were a dream. That girl who was then me.
'My beloved Pritha,' my birth mother would murmur, holding me close to her breasts, overflowing with milk. Even as I reached out to suckle, I was handed away, pushed to the wet nurse. Sweaty, comforting, maternal, she was, unlike my mother, not the sport of kings.

My mother was obsessed with her figure, with the need to stay slim and shapely at any cost. The palace was full of ambitious women casting their eyes at my father, the king Prithibhoja. After every war and skirmish, princesses would be heaped on the palace, trophies of victory, pledges of fearful alliances. It was but natural that my mother should be careful to maintain her beauty, and that she named me Pritha to remind him of their union. My brother was named Vasudeva, a name befitting the future king of the Vrishnis.

Daughters were dispensable: between the fathers and the husbands and the sons, their status was always in flux. Just a year after my birth, I was gifted to my father's cousin Kuntibhoja, as casually as I had been handed over to the wet nurse by my mother. My name was changed as well; I became Kunti, in honour of my new father.

It grieved me that my parents had given me away. I worked hard to earn the love of my foster-parents. Always smiling, full of wise words, even as a child, I became famous for my forbearance. I treasured every nod of approval. If a dog wagged its tail at me, I was grateful for the attention.

At the time of my puberty rites, my birth mother sent me a set of blue and red garments, of soft billowing moonga silk. My adoptive father Kuntibhoja gave me a set of twelve gold bangles, which the river goddess Sona in the northern mountains had gifted to our ancestors.

'Remember, my daughter, that gold becomes purer by the test of fire,' my foster-father said, as he fitted his gift on my wrists. I smiled, pleased, eager to demonstrate my gratitude. I made a resolution, 'I shall submit myself to every test with fortitude,' even as I admired the pure sheen of the bangles.

The rishi Durvasa was to visit our kingdom. The guest from hell. Everyone was in a state of panic, for

Durvasa's irrational rages and irascible curses, irrevocable
because of his penances, wreaked regular devastation
upon his hosts.

'Kunti will attend on the rishi,' my foster-mother
declared, a look of deep satisfaction breaking through
her normally impenetrable face. I did not then understand
that look, I was only grateful to be chosen for such
a difficult task. I oversaw the appointment of the guest
quarters, flowers in bowls, clean sheets. The bathing
pool was scrubbed and scattered with lotus blooms. My
preparations were thorough.

Durvasa was an easy guest, not bad-tempered at
all. 'I cannot suffer fools,' he said, twinkling at me
conspiratorially. 'Every king and prince I meet begs for
a boon: Give me more kingdoms! Grant me a son! Gift me
immortality! My bad temper keeps them away, and if they
persist, I pack them off with a curse as recompense.'
'Such are the ways of kings,' I replied, as neutrally as
I could, and with the modesty for which I was already
famous.

Durvasa was pleased. 'What a sensible young lady we
have here!' he exclaimed. 'I think you deserve a boon. What
is it you would choose? Beauty, fame, wisdom?'
'Whatever you feel a young girl would most enjoy,'
I replied demurely, adjusting my billowing red and
blue skirts.

'The very gods shall be at your command,' Durvasa
declared, his dark eyes flashing with mischief. 'With the

divine magic of this mantra that I now reveal to you, every god and deva from the world beyond shall come to you at your desire, and live on in your bloodline by gifting you his seed.'

'What if I forget the words of the mantra?' I asked anxiously. 'I am only a mortal.'

Durvasa placed his hands on my forehead. His bony knobbly fingers pressed down hard on my skull, so hard that I bit my lips and drew blood. The sacred beeja, the sounds of intent of the mantra, coursed through my body like a revelation, even as the rusty taste of fresh blood filled my mouth.

'We rishis have no need of words, dear child,' Durvasa said, as he removed his hands. 'Do not tell your father or your foster-father of my gift. No one from this palace should know anything of it, or they will try to wrest it from you for their advantage. Carry your courage as proudly as your beauty; in wisdom, you will never be found wanting.' That evening, he strode away from the palace grounds, waving his brass kamandala, carrying away the whiff of forest that his bark robes had brought into the perfumed chambers of the guest quarters.

The king commended me for handling him so well. 'The head gardener claims he saw Durvasa smile,' he said. 'Kunti, you have served our kingdom well.' He was sitting on his throne, his consorts beside him, and the usual gaggle of courtiers and hangers-on in attendance. The chief queen looked sour and said nothing.

Durvasa's visit changed something in me. I no longer
felt the need to please people. 'Carry your courage as
proudly as your beauty,' he had said to me. I began to walk
differently, with my head held high. The women in the
palace noticed the change in my demeanour, and observed
that it was time I was married off. Durvasa's secret mantra
had changed my life.

I, too, was restless for change. I would not sleep all
night, only sigh and long for things I could not understand.
All night, I heard the river murmuring seductively by my
window. Bathed in moonlight, I would watch the waves
playing on the sands of the river Yamuna. She was the river
of destiny for our Vrishni clan, our kingdoms flourished
by her whims. She gave us floods and brought riches to our
soil. Yamuna gave us trade, and when the waters dried up
and the river serpents crawled on to the land, we prayed
for her forgiveness.

The sky had remained sullen all through that monsoon.
It had rained and drizzled for days on end. I had grown
weary of the half-light, and my eyes had tired of the
unvarying expanse of green earth and gray sky outside
my window.
'How I wish the Sun would appear!' I sighed. Just for
practice, I went through the mantra that Durvasa had
imparted to me. The sounds of the invocation fell into
place, vowels following consonants in sonorous ritual
order. In that moment, in the private quarters of the palace,
curtained from the world, a soft light like the first break of
dawn filled up the room. I could sense him beside me, and

then, in a blinding flash of fulfilling glory, I saw Surya, the
god who brings the three worlds to light.
My eyes were dazzled. I saw him, not with my sight, but
with every pore of my being. The light spread and became
a low humming sound. Even as I drowned in that ocean of
incandescent burning, the god surged and swelled inside
me. His lips on mine as tongues of fire devoured my throat.
His seed a burst of life, growing and coming to light. My
womb contracted, first with joy and then with pain. My
eyes were closed but I saw the glory of a thousand suns.
The god departed.

Outside, I could hear the rain beating steadily on the
flagged stones in the central courtyard. There was thunder
and a bolt of lightning filled up the room. The silver
streaks illumined the face of the child emerging through
my parted legs. He examined me with steady eyes, liquid
with trust. Karna, born of my words, seed of Arka whom I
had invoked with the magic of Durvasa's boon. The infant
wore his father's gifts of an invincible armour and a golden
helmet. Gold kundalas hung from his ears, nestling among
the radiant curls that betrayed his divine lineage.
And I, a mortal, was afraid. What explanation would
I give the king and his consorts? What sort of a boon was this?
My son whimpered for milk, and I was glad that the
beating rain masked his cries. My budding breasts swelled
as I fed him, my young nipples hurting as he sucked,
greedily, then contentedly, before he fell asleep.
I placed him in the reed basket that housed my ragged
childhood dolls. Then I went to the courtyard and plucked

some lotus leaves from the pond. The fish rose to nibble my fingers as I broke the mossy stems, one by one, and wiped them on my skirts. It had stopped raining but the sky was still overcast, swollen with the promise of more heavenly tears. I covered my son with the lotus leaves, to protect him from the rain. Then I swaddled him gently in a scarf of orange silk, and walked with light steps to the riverbank. No one, not the royal consorts, nor the handmaidens, would guess my sorrow or my intent from my gait, my demeanor. To them, I was a child still.

I hid behind a bush when I saw the court jester walking moodily along the slushy path to the riverfront. Laughter was his occupation, his duty, but oft-times, he would scowl and growl, then turn unexpectedly gentle. I waited until he had passed and placed the basket with my son in a bank of reeds by the river.

My birth father had named me Pritha. Then, when it was expedient for him to send me away, he had gifted me, as if I were a basket of freshly picked fruit, to his cousin and ally Kuntibhoja. I became Kunti. I became someone who could call the gods. The secret mysteries of dharma are full of summonings and partings.

The sound of distant thunder. The waters were rising steadily. I wept, but the tears did not lighten my heart. The little boat on which I had set my child afloat broke loose of the reeds. It danced joyously with the river currents, and the Yamuna, that sacred and kind-hearted lady, bore him away to his destiny.

I know today that Adiratha the charioteer discovered
the basket as it floated down the river. He rescued my son,
and with his wife Radha reared him as their own.

It is a curse to be born a kshatriya. All this talk of
honour and duty; whose honour is it? Whose duty? I had
borne the seed of the Sun god. My son Karna was noble,
brave and generous. Yet I killed him. Once, and then again.
Whose honour? Whose duty? It was simply fear of being
found disobedient, of disgrace.

❦

All my sons loved me, and I loved them all. Arjuna belonged
to my heart in a way I cannot explain. But of all that I have
loved and lost, my son Karna is the foremost. I see him every
morning, in the reflection of the sun, in the dewdrops that
glisten on the leaves.

It was because I loved him the most that I betrayed him.
In my mother's heart, I had that right. When, deep into the
days of battle, I met Karna and declared our blood bond, I
asked him for the gift of Arjuna's life. With the generosity
of the Sun who gives us life and nourishes all, Karna granted
me my wish. He gave everything away—his armour, his life.
It is not Karna's forgiveness that I seek; he gave me that when
I reclaimed him, to ask him not to fight his brother Arjuna in
battle. It is not my own forgiveness, for I will never grant it.
I seek the mercy of my son's father. The god who filled me
with radiance and granted me a son who was the greatest
warrior ever born. I seek his mercy to redeem me from the
sins and sorrows I bestowed on my firstborn.

We sit together in a grove of pine trees, Gandhari
and I. We have lost our kingdoms, though my sons rule
Hastinapura still. Dhritarashtra and Vidura have gone
for a walk in the forest, Vidura leading his aged, defeated
brother, as spiritually blind as he is physically unable to see,
through the unseen glories of the blooming kadamba trees.
Gandhari is muttering to herself, as usual. The bandage
around her eyes is grimy. Here, in our mountain retreat,
we do not have servants to do our bidding. I shall wash the
bandage in the stream tomorrow.

In a sing-song voice, the queen is intoning the names of
her hundred slaughtered sons. She begins, as usual, with
the eldest, in the order of birth. Gandhari can weep and
mourn her hundred sons, because she did not kill them.
I dare not lament for Karna, even now, except with the
scorched, secret tears of shame when I see the first rays of
the morning reflected on the dewdrops.

As Gandhari mutters and sighs for her hundred sons,
I remain dry-eyed. It is high noon, and the rays of the sun
warm my back in benediction. I was weak when I should
have been strong, afraid of Kuntibhoja and his sour-faced
chief queen. And when the time came to weigh my duty
to myself or to the Pandava clan, I chose but the empty
compulsion of duty. Not the memory of joy.

Writer, publisher and festival director NAMITA GOKHALE is the author
of seven books of fiction and several non-fiction works. Her novels
include *Paro: Dreams of Passion*, *Gods Graves and Grandmother*, *A Himalayan*

Love Story, The Book of Shadows, Shakuntala: the Play of Memory, and *Priya in Incredible Indyaa.* A recent collection of short stories, *The Habit of Love,* (published by Penguin Books India) first carried the 'Kunti' narrative which appears in this collection.

Her engagement with myth and religion is apparent in *The Book of Shiva.* She has retold the *The Mahabharata* in an illustrated version for young and first time readers. *In Search of Sita: Revisiting Mythology,* co-edited with Dr Malashri Lal, presents fresh interpretations of this enigmatic goddess and her indelible impact on the lives of Indian women. Committed to showcasing writing from across the Indian languages, Namita Gokhale is member-secretary of Indian Literature Abroad (ILA), and co-director of the Jaipur Literature Festival and also of the Bhutan literary festival, Mountain Echoes.

Gokhale lives in New Delhi with her mother, and has two daughters and a granddaughter.